SANTONA PUBLICATIONS
2006

MODELLING SCOTLAND'S RAILWAYS

by

IAN FUTERS

First published in 2006
ISBN 0 9538448 8 9
ISBN 978 09538448 8 3

British Library Cataloguing-in-Publication Data. A catalogue record for this book is available from the British Library.

Published by: Santona Publications, Rydal Mount, 224 Marlborough Avenue, Hull. HU5 3LE. **www.santona.co.uk**

Printed by the Amadeus Press, West Yorkshire.
Additional information and copy provided by Ian Fleming and Steve Flint.
Watercolour artwork by Neil A. Ripley.
Scale drawings by the author, Richard Heard and Peter Goss.
Book design and graphics (from author's originals) by Steve Flint.
The author and publisher acknowledge the assistance and support of Peco Publications and Publicity Ltd in the preparation of this book.

Front cover: K2 No. 61788 'Loch Rannoch' (a Fourtrack Models kit) on a short passenger train in this 1950s period view of Loch Lochy.
Title page: Class 25 No. 25303 (a Bachmann Brassworks model) prepares to depart Loch Lochy with a van train in this 1970s scene.
Above: another 1970s scene on Paul Timperley's 4mm scale 'Dalmally' layout, a just-supposing junction for Inverary.

Modelling Scotland's Railways - Contents

Foreword

The great thing about history is there is always one point when it isn't. It is the 'here and now'.

Looking back in railway modelling history one name sticks out as a trailblazer - Ian Futers. I remember seeing Ian's layouts from the very early '80s, when we were all still smitten by pre-war - probably even Edwardian - railways. Ian was modelling what we now call 'modern image'. In reality I do not think that many people actually looked at Ian as a trailblazer, probably because of the things we see around us are those that we take for granted, but all of the modellers 'in the know' knew that what Ian was doing, in modelling terms, really was superb.

He was as skillful and as knowledgeable as any modeller at that time, although his subject was different. It was almost like looking at a Dali picture - you may be confused at the subject, but there was no denying the skill of the execution. I certainly remember Ian's layouts as if they were yesterday, such was their impression on me. At that time I was still modelling pre-First World War, I now find it ironic that, 26 years on, here I am about to model some of the same things that Ian did all that time ago.

There are always people who beaver away and who sometimes do not get the credit they deserve. Ian, because of his chirpy nature and practical joking is one of those characters, so it a pleasure to write the Foreword to a book that should sit on your shelf and rank equally alongside any great modeller who has ever been published.

Pete Waterman
9th May 2006

Pete Waterman is well known as a pop music impresario and lifelong railway enthusiast. Beyond his work in the music industry, he has been involved with numerous railway and railway modelling ventures. Today through his 'Just Like the Real Thing' brand he is spearheading the ultimate in 7mm scale kits of British Railways diesel types as well as numerous steam age prototypes. Visit: **www.justliketherealthing.co.uk** *for further details.*

Chapter 1
A Scottish Layout Portfolio

It will be perhaps interesting to relate how I became captivated by Scottish railways despite never having lived in Scotland. I was born and brought up on Tyneside, which is geographically and socially close to Scotland, but many other influences attracted me to that part of our country.

To begin, my early modelling, typical for one born in the late 1940s, was the usual Hornby 0 Gauge circle of track which included a 'standard' 0-4-0 Hornby tank locomotive in early British Railways livery along with some suburban style four-wheeled coaches. This must have had an early influence on me as I frequently wonder if that rather elementary introduction to railway modelling laid down the roots of my current 7mm interest and also, when constructing my Border branch layouts, I invariably model the early British Railways period,

usually preferring 1953 - the year my dear sister was born!

Sometime later that was followed by an introduction to Hornby-Dublo three-rail when my father built up a system in our garden shed: an old Anderson shelter. This recalls happy Saturday morning visits to Newcastle from Howdon on Tyne, our local station: we would board the North Tyneside electric trains, always alighting at Manors, then walk into town visiting one of the many departmental stores in order to purchase a new wagon or piece of track. Afterwards, there was always a visit to the Grainger Market followed by the return journey from Newcastle Central station.

My father was interested in many things. He was a keen cyclist, which meant, although I never had a new bicycle, our second-hand bikes were always newly painted and well maintained. He

had an interest in photography too, which I like to think he passed onto me. He produced many black and white photographs from the makeshift bathroom dark room. Unfortunately he did not take many railway photographs, apart from a few at nearby Benton Quarry. He also played the saxophone, and most probably scrimped and saved to send me and my brother and sister to piano lessons. For that I am most eternally thankful also. However, most of all, he taught my brother and I many basic handicraft skills including carpentry, soldering and electrical work. These equipped us perfectly for the hobbies we each eventually chose.

I think his own favourite hobby was his gardening. He spent a great deal of time in his beloved greenhouse tending to his seeds and bulbs growing mostly flowers, roses and chrysanthemums. This however, albeit indirectly, changed my

Left: Glen Douglas in 00 gauge was one of my early exhibition layouts. It portrayed a small passing station on the West Highland Railway and was built as a circular layout. (Photograph: the author)

Below: 30 years on, working in a larger scale and I'm still modelling the West Highland. This time representing a short loch side branch terminus in diesel days. The Class 37 model was loaned by DJH. (Photograph: Steve Flint)

Left: it all began here, like many modellers this early layout from the mid 1960s was built up using Triang OO Gauge models and mainly Superquick card kits.
(Photograph: the author)

outlook on railway modelling which was dominated at the time by the Hornby-Dublo three rail. I suppose that was all I really knew then, as for many years my father had purchased the Meccano Magazine each month, but this changed in the Autumn of 1960, and all because of a flower show in our locality. My father belonged to a residents' association in Churchill Street, High Howdon. Each September we would assist him by taking his blooms for the annual flower show, an event which is still held in towns and villages all over the country. That year however, as well as the flower and vegetable show, there was a huge model railway set out in a side room. It was laid out on large boards and consisted of many loops of track with various trains running round. I can remember thinking at the time, 'toy trains'. By the side of the layout were some magazines, unknown to me, entitled 'Railway Modeller'. They were priced at sixpence and I somehow managed to persuade my father to purchase two or three of them. Included in these magazines was an issue, June I think, entitled the 'Peter Denny Special'. Well, after reading these, the monthly purchase of the Meccano Magazine ceased, and the Railway Modeller was purchased each month from then on.

As hinted earlier, this revelation changed my approach to railway modelling - it opened up a huge new world for me.

I was of course aware of the railway network throughout the country, but like many youngsters of the period, my experience of the wider world was very limited. Nowadays, youngsters are seen in main shopping areas as a matter of course, frequently on their own, or with friends, but in contrast, growing up in the 1950s usually meant if you went out anywhere, it was with your parents. Finances were extremely limited and it was not until I became a grocery delivery boy in my mid-teens did I actually have any real money of my own.

However, along with this new introduction to model railways, came another important landmark. My grandfather on my mother's side had a small car, an Austin A30: registration mark UBB 420! He and my grandmother would frequently take me out on trips, invariably at the weekend. Our visits were to the well know beauty spots in Northumberland, usually Bolam Lakes and Rothbury. My brother rarely came with us and my sister would have only been very young. One day we must have traversed mid-Northumberland until we were on the minor road leading from Scotsgap up to Rothbury itself. The road passed over the Rothbury branch at Longwitton and I can still remember seeing the station, and the unfamiliar concrete sleepers which were at that location. This must have set me off thinking as to where this railway originated and where did it go to?

Despite many visits to Rothbury at that time, I never did visit Rothbury station, and it was to be a number of years before I visited Longwitton again.

On that occasion there were no tracks to be seen. However, about the same time we used to have infrequent family holidays in Alston and during one such visit, I must have been in my early teens, I borrowed my father's camera and recorded the station remains in full. This must have been a 'defining moment' with regard to my modelling interests and in particular, a new level of interest in structures required at stations.

By now I was attending the Hadrian Secondary Modern School and, along with two or three of my friends, was dabbling in model railways. I was making up track with the Peco spiked track kits. The Peco Streamline range was just coming onto the market then, though it seemed to take an age for the matching Streamline points to arrive in the shops! My usual model shop was the Whitley Model Shop in Park View, Whitley Bay.

It was now 1965, and the Youth Employment Service of the day threw me into the world of business and commerce. I commenced work at Thermal Syndicate in Wallsend, a company which at the time produced silica products and high temperature glassware for laboratories. I worked in the Costs Office. During this period I had a trackside pass for the Newcastle to Carlisle line, photographing the stations and met up with the late Alan Cook, who also worked at Thermal in the Chemistry Laboratory. He introduced me to finer standards of modelling and we both became members of the LNER Society, as it was then known. Alan was instrumental in helping me out with many projects at the time and I learnt a great deal from him. In 1968, I left Thermal Syndicate to attend Northern Counties Teacher Training College in Benton, Newcastle. This was yet another change of direction, which was to result in my chosen career of teaching very young children.

In terms of my hobby, this was to be quite an important stage in my modelling development. I lost interest in the endless running of Tri-ang locomotives and rolling stock around circles of track, and from reading articles in the model press,

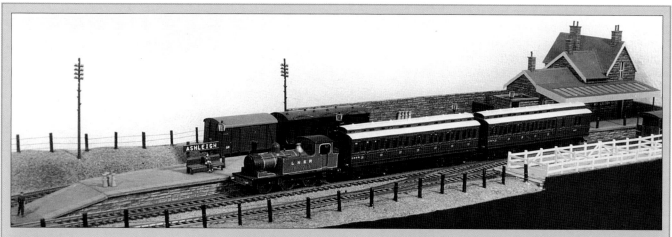

Ashleigh

This was my first exhibition layout built in 1971. A conventional branch terminus track plan, but one that was built quickly using proprietary items of the day. What would the result be like, I wonder, if it was recreated using all the fine models available now? *(Photograph: the author)*

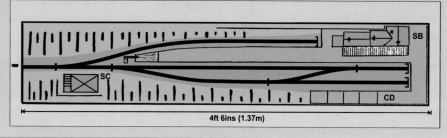

4ft 6ins (1.37m)

I developed an interest in branch lines and the more realistic aspects of layout building. I still feel my Tri-ang and Superquick building days were extremely useful as they taught me many basic skills required to produce layouts. I was moving away from the 'train set' period, though for the time being I was still working in 'OO' scale, and during an Easter vacation in 1971, just before I completed my teacher training, I constructed my first branch terminus, a layout called Ashleigh.

At the time I was vaguely modelling the LNER period, mainly I suppose due to Alan Cook's influence; however, the station building had been inspired by a Scottish prototype, Innerleithen, on the Peebles line. This then brought me into contact with the pre-grouping companies and in particular the North British Railway. From reading the limited accounts at the time, I found that the NBR had greatly influenced the rural railways of Mid-Northumberland. And so began an interest that has remained with me to this day.

Ashleigh was also the first layout I exhibited, at a Newcastle show in the Civic Centre. This layout was eventually published in the September 1972 issue of the Railway Modeller and has apparently encouraged many other modellers to

have a go at producing their first small layout. I suppose I was destined to be intrinsically linked with the design and construction of small layouts from then on. Though, in actual fact, I have never been in a situation to construct very large layouts due to the constraints of space and finances, not an unusual combination. First of all I was living at home with my parents and sharing a bedroom with my brother. My early ventures into property purchasing were limited to quite small houses with little spare space for layout building, except in the garage. It was only when I moved to rural Norfolk that I was finally in a position to purchase a more substantial property; yet even now I cannot seem to find the need to fill spare rooms with model railways. A music room yes, but not model railways! These are still to be found along one wall of the garage, with some additional storage in a garden shed.

During the three years I was at teacher training college, two or three other events shaped the way my modelling was to evolve. I opted to travel away for each of my teaching practices, twice to Scotland and once to Cumbria. In Scotland I had my first teaching practice near to Kelso and later, my final practice in Hawick. This was to initiate a long association with the Borders and of

course a wider study of the North British Railway and other Scottish lines. It was during 1971 when I worked in Hawick where my digs overlooked the station. The Waverley route had just been closed and was then being ruthlessly dismantled. Fortunately, I managed to take a few photographs of the station including a green 08 hauling the contractor's trains.

After training, my teaching career commenced in Whitley Bay and brought with it a bit more finance and my first new car. Prior to that, I had had a number of old 'bangers' which really were not to be trusted on longish trips. So now, visits to other model railway shows started, as well as visits by rail to other destinations further afield. One of these expeditions was to Fort William and Mallaig, a trip that was inspired by a photograph in the book by John Thomas on the West Highland Railway. The photograph in question was that of a K1 leaving the old Fort William station. The issue for me was the simplicity of the station. I wanted to see for myself if indeed the station consisted of two turnouts? And yes, it did only consist of two turnouts. From then on a love affair with Fort William and the West Highland Railway began, one which has, for over thirty five years, been shared with my passion for the Border Branches.

Numerous layouts have been produced over those years and apart from a change of direction to include three Austrian layouts, they have all usually been set either in the Borders, on the West Highland or, at a later stage, in South East Northumberland. Many of these later layouts have been fictitious schemes linked to possible North British routes: the link to the North British is usually included somewhere! Quite naturally, most have been based on the prototypical simple and smallish track plans that were used, and because many of the Border branches, especially those in Northumberland, operated ex-North Eastern Railway locomotives, my locomotive collection had to utilise such stock. In a similar vein, as I have mentioned, my steam style layouts are usually based on the early 1950s, so ex-LNER locomotives have had to be constructed as well. As an aside here, when I model the diesel era, I tend to concentrate on the 'blue period', although of late I have been attracted to the bright Scotrail and Strathclyde liveries. As I hope to show, there is plenty of scope in modelling the railways of Scotland in whatever period you are interested.

After Ashleigh, and the visit to Fort William, I was quite smitten with the West Highland line. A further visit to Scotland in my new Fiat 500 took me, albeit slowly, by the side of Loch Long up to Glen Douglas, as well as a foray up to Ardlui. Both these locations prompted me to construct 4mm layouts in the early 1970s. The first, Glen Falloch, was a fictitious station based on Ardlui and this too was exhibited at Newcastle. It was a large layout and suffered from a lack of suitable rolling stock. On the other hand, Glen Douglas (above right) evolved in the form of a complete circle, quite novel at the time but in actual fact, the total length of the scenic area was slightly more than if it had been built in the standard oval style of the period. There were to be further 'donut' styled layouts later on, as we shall see.

Whilst Ashleigh had been constructed using Peco Streamline track, Glen Falloch and Glen Douglas were both constructed in 00, but this time using 4mm finescale trackwork. The structures on the layout were all scaled from measurements taken on the field trip. I also

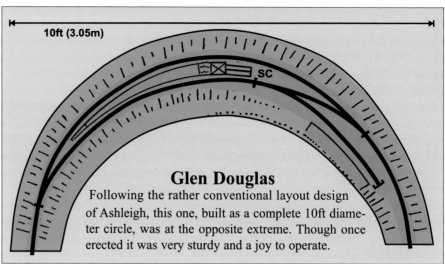

10ft (3.05m)

SC

Glen Douglas

Following the rather conventional layout design of Ashleigh, this one, built as a complete 10ft diameter circle, was at the opposite extreme. Though once erected it was very sturdy and a joy to operate.

operated Glen Douglas in the true North British period. The GEM NBR kits for the Glens were available then, and quite a number of these were constructed to represent other similar Reid classes. A good friend of mine at the time was Dave Alexander of North Shields. He built me a B1, based upon the Jamieson kit, and a scratch built K4. For some reason the layout was invited to the Harrogate Show, my first exhibition away from Tyneside. I met many new friends that weekend including a very youthful Mike Cook from York. I remember I badgered him to invite Glen Douglas to the 1976 York Show, which he did, and so commenced a good friendship, like so many within the hobby, which has lasted for thirty years or more.

During the mid 1970s I began more serious and rewarding research into the three ex-NBR lines in Northumberland. Apart from a small book by Chris Warn, a geography teacher in Northumberland, very little was written about the routes and it was not surprising that a few historical anomalies crept in as a consequence, especially regarding dates. A few photographs existed, and whilst a certain amount of information could be gathered from the Northumberland Records Office, personal site visits proved the most fruitful. Many were made with a couple of like-minded souls and photographs were taken along the Border Counties, Wansbeck and Rothbury lines. Even today, I just have to be within sight of that area and all the memories return. It was, of course, inevitable that a layout would emerge, in fact more than one did. The first layout to appear was Saughtree

and it coincided with my adopting EM gauge standards. Saughtree was a very small station just inside Scotland on the Border Counties line. It was then followed by Middleton North on the Wansbeck line; this layout was quite a large affair despite the station consisting of only a single siding. Further cast kits were constructed in order to expand the locomotive stud, many by necessity being of North Eastern origin. As mentioned earlier, the Northumbrian branches had, since LNER days, been operated with ex-North Eastern stock; fortunately the 4mm Nu-Cast range was being introduced during that period.

The trilogy was completed with a model of Longwitton, taken from the Rothbury branch. This was again built as a circular layout, like Glen Douglas, a style I quite favour. All these layouts were constructed in EM Gauge, but I was already looking towards building layouts in the newly emerging scale/gauge standard of 18.83mm, or P4 as it has become better known.

I had been working away on a project based on a fictitious line that would end up at Otterburn in North Northumberland. I spent a lot of time in research, checking gradient profiles and the locations of bridges, to ensure that such a line could have been constructed from Woodburn station on the Wansbeck line. The layout appeared in 1979 and was one of the first such layouts in P4 to be shown on the exhibition circuit. (see chapter 3) It appeared at many shows, including three or four venues around London in the space of six or seven weeks. By the time it made its final appearance, it was

Longwitton

The prototype of this delightful little halt on the Rothbury branch is shown right, c.1955. My 1977 model, below, was constructed in circular format, although the plan shows how it could be built straight in just 7ft in 4mm scale.

(Photographs: the author, right: A. J. Wickens)

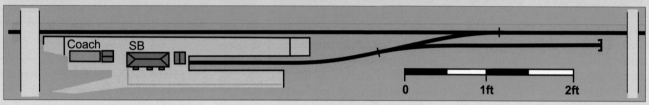

quite worn out, but many valuable lessons had been learnt. In particular it taught me to always put in additional wiring at rail joints in order to ensure good power continuity. This is something I still do today, it only takes an afternoon or so to fit the wiring, but peace of mind is then always there.

The next P4 layout I sprung onto an unsuspecting public was in late 1980. This layout was operated with diesel power and was once again another of those 'just supposing' style of layouts. That is to say, the locations were ficti-

Below: my 4mm Lochside layout appeared in 1980 and was possibly one of the first P4 layouts to feature diesels. Apparently it inspired quite a few modellers to consider diesels, but dyed-in-the-wool steam-age modelling friends thought I'd lost the plot! See photographs on page 48 and 59.

tious, but they had to have a suitable history and the rolling stock had to be typical of the area and period modelled. That layout was, of course, Lochside and it seemed to cause a sensation because of the diesels and the fact it was reasonably in the 'modern image'. Many people did not realise at the time that I was photographing modern stock and in particular examples found in Scotland. During the long school holidays, a group of us would leave Tyneside early on in the morning and spend a full day up in Scotland visiting the major depots. The result is a huge library of black and white negatives of Class 06s, 08s, 20s, 25s, 26s and 27s. Other types were covered including the Deltics, but my main interest was in what most people considered the more mundane classes.

The diesels for Lochside were all

based upon examples found at Eastfield depot in Glasgow and therefore could have quite easily visited the West Highland line.

Many of the locomotives I have constructed over the years have been built with more than one layout in mind. This still happens today, as astute modellers will realise from looking at the numbers on my locomotives! It is also a good way of stopping you purchasing some of the more interesting items the trade introduces from time to time.

It is interesting to note that my main interests over the years have remained with the West Highland and the Borders. Thus the theme of building small, highly detailed layouts continued into the more modern diesel period. The focus was still the same, that is to say, decide on the area of interest then initiate research into

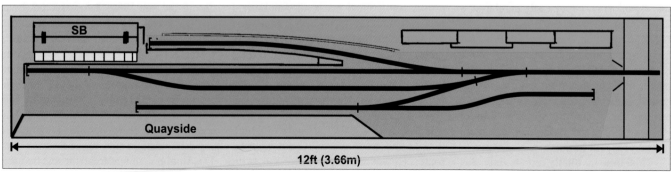

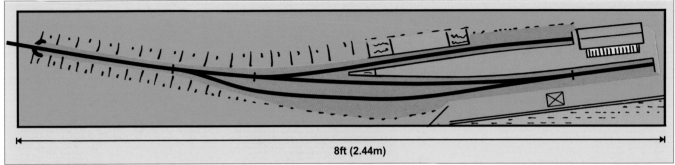

8ft (2.44m)

structures and buildings as well as developing a modicum of plausible historical accuracy. Rolling stock details could be easily sourced, usually by on-site observations or through the invaluable Ian Allan locomotive books. Once these factors have been observed, and closely adhered to, an accurate portrayal could be established and modelled.

After Lochside, a slight amount of turmoil entered my life and for some forgotten reason I embarked upon another P4 layout, this time of Scotsgap Junction on the Wansbeck line. This was a huge layout with eleven turnouts and to this day I can only vaguely remember why I built it. I suppose I was tagged with a label that indicated I only built layouts with two or three turnouts, and so wanted to prove I could build something slightly larger. This of course is quite true but Scotsgap did not stay in one piece for long. During all my period of turmoil, I had been studying at Newcastle University for a second degree. This degree was linked to my interest in rural education and rural primary schools. After gaining my B.Phil. degree, to complement my Open University B.A., I departed from Tyneside in the summer of 1984 and took up my first Headship at Priors Marston First School, which was a small and attractive village school in rural Warwickshire.

With a totally new environment and indeed new life in Warwickshire, I did a lot of exploring. I eventually purchased a house within sight and sound of the GWR main line between Oxford and Leamington Spa, quite a culture shock really. Naturally my new job and the responsibilities that went with it took up quite a bit of my time. However, I soon joined the Leamington Spa Model Railway Club, and thoughts once again turned to layout building.

This time a totally urban line was produced in P4 named Burnfoot, which had an island platform surrounded by retaining walls and factory units. The urban theme had been slowly developing during my year out at Newcastle University, when I would travel into the city using the Metro system. During the same period I had also travelled extensively around the country by train (complete with a student railcard!) and observed many urban scenes. The name of the layout actually came from an estate in Hawick, where I did my final teaching practice in 1971. It was similar to Lochside, based somewhere in Glasgow and the Eastfield diesels were once again utilised. The layout was built at some speed and used trackwork made up entirely of copper-clad sleepers. I was invited to take the layout to shows in new areas, a direct result of working with the Leamington club. At this point I also became the exhibition manager of the club and I like to feel the little one day show in the Spring blossomed into one of those 'must attend' type of shows. Certainly we invited some of the most well known layouts of the time with attendances topping 2500 one year.

The second layout to be built in Warwickshire saw me return to a theme which had been festering in my mind for quite some time. I had read articles about, and been intrigued by, a small rural line in Fife: the freight only line to Lochty. I added a station building to allow a passenger service and Lochend was born. I was still working in P4 and I alternated the operation between steam and early green diesels. This was exhibited during the mid 1980s and coincided with a house move to a small village on the border between Northamptonshire and Warwickshire named Staverton. Again it was nearby to a main line, only this time it was the now closed Great Central route. However, it provided me with

Above: In the mid 1980s I built this simple terminus based on the freight only Lochty branch in Fife, though I added a station building for passenger traffic. This was 'Lochend' which was set in the 1950s and ran with both ex-NBR steam locos and green diesels. The Lochty branch has always been one of my favourites and is dealt with in much greater detail in Chapter 6, along with a photograph of this layout on page 65.

some interesting walks and allowed me once again to explore an almost forgotten railway, but this time a main line. It so happened that after a short period in the village, I was appointed as Head to Staverton Primary School, commencing duties in the September of 1990. I lived opposite the school itself, although this is something I would not normally consider or recommend!

For a number of years I had been visiting Austria for holidays and had met up on several occasions with a good friend, Ernst Wolf from Gmunden. I had first become acquainted with Ernst in 1979. He has since presented me with his 35mm slide collection consisting of over 5000 European railway slides. He lives in the Salzkammergut region, which just happened to have a gorgeous single track cross country line running through it - shades of the Border Counties Railway really. I had shunned all things Continental for many years, but the continual visits to the region won me over and so during the late 1980s I constructed three layouts based upon Austrian practice. They were, in order of construction, Traunsee, a large continuous run layout named after a lake in the Salzkammergut and then Altaussee, a small branch terminus named after a village in the south of the region. The final Austrian layout was a town terminus using an elevated position and named Neumarkt. This final layout was to be the test bed for a P4 layout, which was to influence a whole host of projects in the 1990s.

I ceased working with Austrian layouts in the early 1990s although my interests in matters European still continue to this day and many of my holidays include the opportunity to photograph the railways of the countries I visit. I have quite a fascination with Eastern Europe and Scandanavia and as well as meeting Ernst Wolf in Austria, I now have friends in Spain and the Czech Republic. In the latter, my friend Tomas Studnicka assists me with visits to Poland and other countries in the East. Once again, a vast collection of negatives has built up. However, I digress, in railway modelling matters the early days of the 1990s saw me changing direction once again and moving up into the senior scale: 7mm/ft.

At first, this consisted of constructing three or four diesels from etched or white metal kits. They were again all Eastfield based prototypes and a small locomotive stabling point called 'Lochty Road' (right) was developed. Although it proved a large, cumbersome layout to transport, it was enjoyable to work in the larger scale. At the same time I started building up a small collection, in 7mm scale, of typical locomotives found on the Northumbrian branch lines. Alan Cook once again assisted me considerably with these locomotives, although the intention was to have them sitting in a glass case, rather than build a layout for them.

By now it was 1993 and I once again wanted to expand my career in education. I applied for the Headship of a town school, Swaffham First School in Norfolk. It was a much larger school but I still considered it to be in a rural setting and there were huge possibilities to be initiated at such a large establishment. So again everything was packed up, Lochty Road was sold, and a new life commenced in East Anglia. Now, I have always enjoyed Arthur Ransome's books, so I looked forward to being able to explore, in great depth, the places in that area that he noted in his works.

At the same time, a P4 layout based upon the concept of the Austrian town

Right: several of my layouts have been built on the basis that the North British Railway did, in fact, get into Newcastle. 'Newcastle NB' set in the 1950s, was one such 7mm/ft essay. *(Photograph: the author)*

Lochty Road
This layout, my first venture into 0 Gauge, was built and exhibited during 1991. The locomotives were built from the original Parkin Kits and are made of etched brass and whitemetal. The scenics, as usual, were quite minimal, with just a stabling shed, fueling point and small locomens' office.
(Photograph: the author)

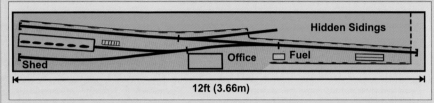

terminus had taken shape, and by the time I moved over to Norfolk, it was complete and working a good four months before its first outing. This was Newcastle (Haymarket), an ultra-small town terminus based upon what an actual NBR station in Newcastle might have looked like: in fact its intended setting was close to the location where one had been proposed in the 1880s.

I operated this layout with new P4 stock comprising of diesel multiple units with the odd parcels working to give a bit of variation. The layout was extremely well detailed, an elevated terminus station, and I really enjoyed working it. It attended quite a number of exhibitions and is still to be seen on the circuit as I

write. People frequently ask what happens to my old layouts. Well the most recent ones have been sold on, but in the early days they would be stripped of working parts and then frequently thrown on the council tip!

I have mentioned that the Austrian /Newcastle Haymarket configuration was to be used again. The next layout to appear was the 7mm version of Haymarket: so much for keeping the 7mm locomotives in the display cabinet! The same trackplan was used but the layout was built into a cutting, surrounded by retaining walls and over-bridges. Because I had pre-dated the layout back to the early 1950s, I called it Newcastle N.B., (below). The small locomotive stud

St Catherine's for Loch Fyne

Although my ultimate aim is to construct the original terminus at Fort William, I could not resist constructing this might-have-been style of layout based upon the proposal to reach Loch Fyne and St Catherine's from Arrochar and Tarbet. A close look at the track plan will reveal a similar configuration to my three point sagas based on Tyneside. The passenger service was based very loosely on the Arrochar to Craigendoran push-pull set which ran for many years with an ex-NBR 4-4-2T, an example of which is shown here. See also pages 74 and 81 for some more views of this layout.

(Photograph: the author)

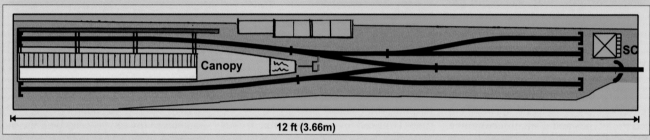

Canopy

12 ft (3.66m)

had been added to with a selection of non-corridor coaching stock and parcels vehicles. However, the historical assumptions were still adhered to, assuming that the NBR had constructed such a station in Newcastle and all the NBR services used the station to service the routes to Rothbury, Scotsgap and Hawick. The locomotives were all modelled on examples known to have worked the Northumbrian branches.

This was followed with yet another small depot style layout, this time using the collection of 7mm steam locomotives which was steadily growing as my interest in the scale developed. The depot was called Cold Harbour Lane, which had nothing whatsoever to do with the North East or Scotland. It was named after a song, but in fact such a lane is to be found within a mile of my house in Norfolk. The layout had been constructed as a small 'interim' project style layout whilst larger plans, featuring a proposed branch line off the West Highland line at Arrochar, developed.

A visit to Scotland in the summer of 1999 rekindled my interest in matters West Highland. I was astonished to recall that it had been over fifteen years since I had last visited the area, but apart from rolling stock and signalling, little else seemed to have changed. I also visited

Fort William and took my first good look at the new station there. I made myself a promise to visit other parts of the line and the seeds were sown for a series of articles in the 'Railway Modeller' called 'West Highland Wanderings'.

However, the line which initially interested me was a little known project to build a railway from Arrochar to St Catherines, a small hamlet on the east shore at the head of Loch Fyne. The line had been proposed as a light railway in the late 1890s but was never built. The gradients would have been extremely fierce, but that did not stop me adopting the history to enable a model on a small loch side location. The layout was to have a very grand title, probably the longest station name I have ever used, St Catherine's for Loch Fyne. It was quite a compact layout, still using the Haymarket style of track plan but with an added carriage siding and, as a backdrop, a stone 'storm' wall, which I like to think had a look of Mallaig about it. It also saw me using a new set of locomotives which included a K1 and a K4 along with an ex-NBR C15 with two suburban coaches like those on the Arrochar to Craigendoran push pull set. When a number of fish vans made their appearance, I realised that the lure of the West Highland line was as strong as ever.

Nevertheless, West Highland matters were put on a hold after that layout, because in order to build the layout I was still aspiring to (and more of that later) there was the little matter of building up the correct rolling stock for it. It was now the late twentieth century, and an exciting period for Scottish 7mm modellers, as many prototypes were being produced, or promised, in the senior scale. I continued my policy of purchasing only the items I required for future projects. Though to be honest I had quite a few themes pencilled out on scraps of paper, including a number of projects set in the Borders, of lines which had never been constructed for one reason or another - usually because of the lack of finance, but I always find these 'just supposing' projects extremely interesting.

However, the next layout saw a return to an urban terminus in Newcastle. I had discovered that the NBR had indeed planned to assist with the building of a new line through mid Northumberland and into Scotland in the late 1880s. Their terminus was to be in Percy Street, just yards from my previous Newcastle Haymarket and N.B. creations, which had been located close to the actual Haymarket area of the town. The trusty old three-turnout composition appeared again and Percy Street was created,

initially in ScaleSeven. After about two shows the trackwork was converted back to 32mm (0 gauge), but not because the ScaleSeven standards were difficult to achieve. The layout ran very well, and I really enjoyed making the trackwork, but it was more to do with drastic conversion work necessary to the Bachmann 7mm diesels: something I was not too keen to continue with. However, my good friend and travelling operator Steve Corrigall, who still lives on Tyneside, dropped a bombshell during one show and suggested my modelling had become quite stale with these small terminus style layouts based in Newcastle. Now, the price of an honest friend may be rubies, but…

Just to prove Steve and perhaps others wrong, I embarked on yet another layout which returned to the Lochside theme: and so the 7mm version of Lochside appeared during 2002 (above). It had an additional siding space to the earlier 4mm version as well as a small stabling depot, so consequently many hours of shunting were possible. It was set in the late 1970s/early 1980s period enabling fish traffic to be just plausible (the 'Wick Fish' van service finished in 1981). Many visitors would reminisce about the original Lochside, some even brought photographs to show their own versions. However, it was an absolute beast to transport round. One could say it was a good thing I had moved on from the Fiat 500, but once the layout had been fitted in the car, it was impossible to see out of the rear window or even the passenger side window. Every available

amount of space in the trusty VW Golf was used up. If I had to pick up Steve at, say Peterborough, he had to shoehorn himself into the passenger seat and usually had a stock box on his lap!

After a particularly nasty weekend health-wise at a northern exhibition during the Autumn of 2002, (I contracted pneumonia, apparently), I withdrew Lochside from the exhibition circuit and put it up for sale. I spent the whole of 2003 plotting and planning a new smaller layout, whilst still putting together the pieces for my magnum opus layout which was requiring all of this new stock. 'That Project' was actually started during that year and is currently snaking down one side of the garage. It is, of course, Fort William, and at the time of writing, the station throat with its two curved turnouts and the two beautiful signals, are up and working. The layout lacks scenic detail, apart from the sturdy retaining wall next to what will be Loch Linnhe. It will probably remain in that state until all the locomotives are completed and the coaching stock too. There will be lots of Gresleys and Thompsons, with one or two BR Mark 1s. I have set the period for Fort William as 1953, Coronation year, and, as I have mentioned earlier, the year my dear sister was born!

Realising that my Fort William layout will have a long period of gestation, I wanted something to keep me on the exhibition circuit. That invariably means a smallish project and one that resulted in a return to yet another of my favourite subjects: the Northumbrian branches.

They still hold a great fascination for me, and, in time I am sure I will construct a layout based upon Kielder Forest. The thought of Scottish class 4-4-0s with two or three coaches; or the SO Hexham to Kielder one-coach service along with the bonus goods service, is simply too delightful, in my opinion, to overlook. In the meantime however, that next layout was a mixture of two Northumbrian stations. One end had the platform and station building of Woodburn, whilst the other end had the loading bank and road bridge as found at Kielder. The resulting layout was christened Otterburn, and when it first appeared in 2004 the response was the same as when Lochside reappeared: much reminiscing and pleasure at seeing me return to my roots - the NBR branch lines in Northumberland. Once again it was a layout with limited operation. Following its first couple of outings the sector plate was lengthened in order to make the shunting a little easier. This illustrates a case in point: sometimes all the planning in the world will not aid a layout until it is actually up and working and you have been physically able to try out all the moves. In this case we discovered we needed somewhere to store the brake van and that was why the sector plate had to be lengthened. The locomotive could now fully run round its train in order to carry out the shunting of the sidings. It proves a theory I have about railway modelling which roughly translates into 'you are never too old to learn something of use'.

That actually brings us right up to date with the history of my layouts. One or two have been omitted because they were only exhibited once or twice and never actually made the modelling press. These included Deadwater (EM), a Border Counties line station on the border itself; Angerton (P4) a passing station on the Wansbeck line, this was only exhibited twice but actually still survives now as an LNWR terminus! (see page 31). A second version of Glen Falloch (P4) appeared in the mid 1980s, but it too only appeared twice at exhibitions,

13

mainly because I was concentrating on the P4 Otterburn project. I once had the baseboards constructed for a P4 version of Kielder Forest too, but it was never completed. For anyone interested in the Border Counties line, I have included my original scale drawings of the buildings at Deadwater, along with a layout plan at the bottom of the page.

During the 1970s and 1980s it seemed as though I produced a new layout each year, but in actual fact I frequently used to have more than one project on the go at any one time!

I still work like that, and hopefully as this tome reaches the bookshelves, a couple of new layouts featured within these pages will be on the exhibition circuit. One is an urban terminus, based upon an actual location near to central Glasgow. Its name is Victoria Park and it may eventually be operated as a current Scotrail style of layout (see page 56). There is just a slight problem of sourcing suitable modern 7mm rolling stock, especially second generation DMUs, though kits are available from a couple of small manufacturers The second layout has a West Highland theme and is based on a proposed branch from Spean Bridge into the Great Glen which was included in the original West Highland Act of 1884, but removed so as not to upset the Highland Railway! This is Loch Lochy and has just embarked on the exhibition circuit this very year (2006)

As someone who has constructed many, many layouts, all mostly quite small affairs, I still hold great admiration for those modellers who have stuck with one particular subject and set out to model it as accurately as possible and to the best of their ability. I know modellers who have painstakingly researched a particular line, constructed a layout on it and built the associated stock for it: but it has taken them decades to achieve it. A noble objective perhaps, and in contrast, it might seem to some that I have fluttered about when building my own layouts, but I can say with a clear conscience that I have remained true to the cause: apart from the Continental hiccup, I have always concentrated on the two locations which I feel I have researched well and portrayed accurately; namely the Border branches and the West Highland route and its associated branches.

The lines built or planned in Northumberland were, in the days just before they closed to passenger traffic, restricted to perhaps a G5 0-4-4T and a J21 0-6-0, along with a coach or two. Slightly larger locomotives operated over the Border Counties line, but there was little in the way of variation. In contrast on the West Highland, there is much greater scope for a variety of interesting stock items. For instance, if you model it in the LNER or British Railways period, you can have a wide selection of Gresley or Thompson locomotives and coaches, as well as both ex-LMS and BR Standard types. As the West Highland lines in the main survived the Beeching cuts, you can therefore utilise the diesel classes that worked the routes. Although variety of type was less, the mid-powered Sulzer classes that were the mainstay for nearly twenty years were the most attractive of diesel types in my opinion. And because the original West Highland infrastructure has more or less remained the same for years, it is easy to gather the correct prototype information for practically any period you want to model.

Now before moving on, one or two readers out there are maybe wondering how the County of Northumberland fits into the Scottish railways theme. The North British Railway, firmly a Scottish company with headquarters in Edinburgh, had the city of Newcastle in its sights for many a year and did eventually gain running powers into the magnificent Newcastle Central Station. However, it was at quite a great cost. The actual lines they had helped to come to fruition within the county eventually became rural backwaters, along with a meandering cross country route into Scotland itself. However they served their communities well, until closure in the early and mid 1950s. That apart, Northumberland and a little part of Cumbria are included because I decided to use as 'The Border', a line that roughly follows the route of Hadrian's Wall: the Roman border of antiquity between England and Scotland. Also, the Border Marches were for many centuries a disputed region between the two countries. The various warring factions fought for English, Scottish and frequently purely selfish reasons often related to matters pertaining to sheep! As a result, Scottish and English cultures and their economies are invariably intertwined across the region. And if all that doesn't justify the inclusion of Northumberland, I can also point out that the geological boundary between Scotland and England follows the Whin Cill fault line which runs from the Tyne Estuary in the East to the Solway Firth in the West. The numerous rocky cliff outcrops of the Whin Cill also provided natural ramparts upon which Hadrian's Wall was built: so with all those factors in place, I rest my case…

Speaking of historical matters, that is where we must go first, because an understanding of a railway's social, economic and technical history will surely assist us in building models that are interesting, accurate and authentic.

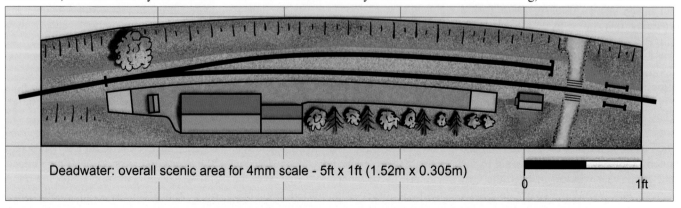

Deadwater: overall scenic area for 4mm scale - 5ft x 1ft (1.52m x 0.305m)

0   1ft

Deadwater Station Buildings

Scale 2mm = 1ft (1:152)

20ft 10ft 0

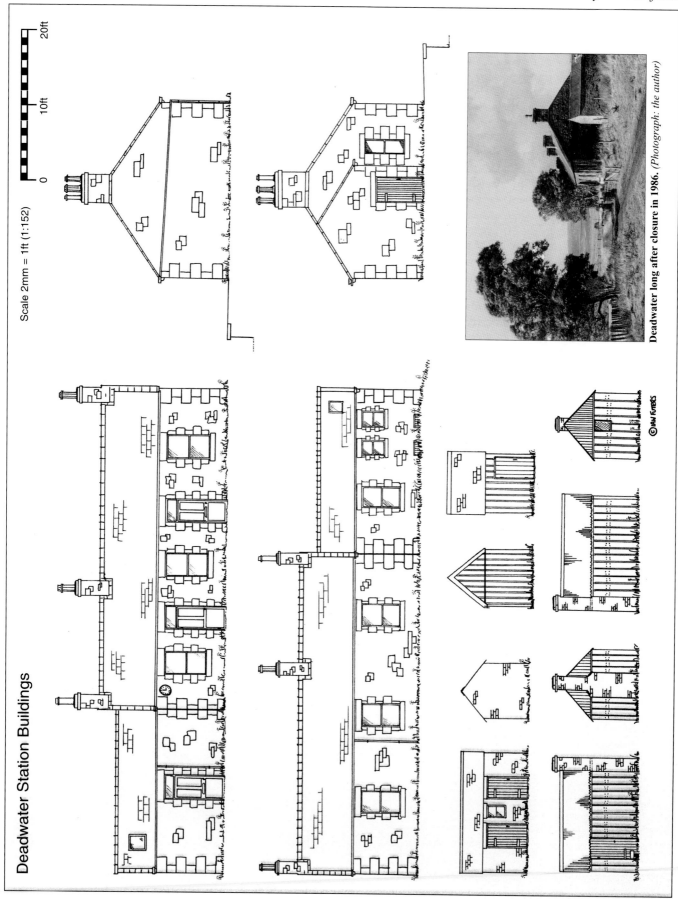

Deadwater long after closure in 1986. *(Photograph: the author)*

© IAN FUTERS

Chapter 2

Quintessentially Scottish Railways

As with many areas in the United Kingdom, the railways in Scotland were built as a means of transporting raw materials or finished goods from a mineral source, or factory, to the customer. Many of the early railways were simple wagon-ways, which allowed the goods to be delivered frequently to nearby canals or ports. Quite a number of these wagon-ways, and associated ports, were owned by illustrious landowners or particular companies, and rich profits could be made. With the advent of steam power, locomotives could be made to run along the tracks of the wagon-ways. Over a short period of time numerous concerns were soon operating these as true early railways, and invariably some were amalgamated into larger companies.

It is not my intention to write at length about each individual railway company or how and when amalgamations took place; that itself would take up a book or two. In any case, we are looking specifically at how to make authentic models of these locations as there have been many books published over the years on the individual companies.

Below: Glen Douglas was one of the few layouts I built portraying Scotland's pre-grouping railways. The locomotives were from the GEM range of kits, some of which are still available. *(Photograph: author)*

Indeed, there have also been many specialised books published, quite often on a very local basis, about the railways of a particularly small geographical area. Frequently, these can only be sourced in local bookshops and libraries in the area, although it is easier these days to trace publications through the Internet.

As intimated, many of the early lines were absorbed into larger concerns and eventually five particular companies formed the overall structure of Scottish railways. They were; the North British Railway, the Caledonian Railway, the Glasgow & South Western Railway, the Highland Railway and the Great North of Scotland Railway. There was of course intense rivalry between these companies, not only for traffic but also for the prestige of being the 'best' in Scotland. This rivalry extended to the corporate image of each company, they all had very distinctive liveries and house styles. Railway staff in particular, remained extremely loyal to the company they worked for and I am led to believe through hearsay, that this traditional rivalry still exists in certain parts of the railway network of Scotland today!

With reference to the map opposite, I will show the geographical areas where the five pre-grouping companies operated. Obviously there were some joint lines

where stock from two or three companies could be found, and this continued, even when in 1923, the five companies were amalgamated to form part of two distinctive national companies; the London and North Eastern Railway (LNER) and the London, Midland and Scottish Railway (LMS). In 1947 these two companies, under nationalisation, became the Scottish Region of British Railways. This in turn became British Rail, Scottish Region, then Scotrail and now, under privatisation, at the time of writing, First Scotrail. However, when travelling around Scotland by rail today, it is still quite easy to identify the 'house styles' of the five pre-grouping companies and, in many instances, their earlier constituent companies as well: a legacy indeed from Victorian and Edwardian times.

Accordingly, this chapter is intended as a brief insight into the quintessential features of each of the five railway companies that shaped the Scottish Railway scene. Other than for very recent times, modellers aiming for the authentic look can see at a glance what the typical architecture was like, or, was likely to have been at the location of their layout. Useful possibly to modellers less familiar with Scottish railways who prefer the 'just supposing' approach to layout design and construction.

As I stated earlier, my own particular interest was rooted at a very early age, although I do not suppose I was aware of it at the time. I still remember travelling across a railway line in Northumberland whilst out with my grandparents at the age of about eleven. Many years later I

found out that this was the Northumberland Central Railway built in the 1860s and 1870s and known locally as the Rothbury Branch. I also found out that although it started out as a local line, funded by local people, the mighty North British Railway based in Edinburgh

assisted with its construction. Further investigation revealed that the NBR had an interest in the line because they wanted to gain a foothold in Newcastle itself in order to consolidate their 'empire' as it were. The progression I took in favouring the North British as my

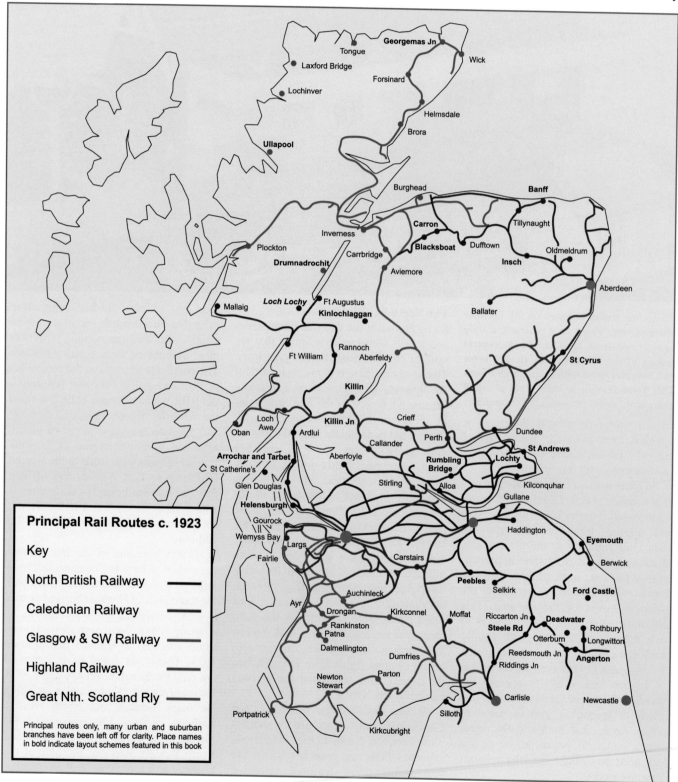

Above: the station buildings on my Lochside schemes were based on Eyemouth, a style used at numerous locations on the central section of the North British, though some had canopies fitted with small porch wings. This 7mm version is built from plywood and plastic sheet. *(Photograph: the author)*

chosen prototype should therefore be obvious, even from the tender age of eleven! I am fairly sure many modellers can associate with this approach.

In order to model an accurate portrayal of a station or line, I think an interest in a particular company is usually essential, and applies from the pre-grouping companies right up to the present day. Modellers of the current scene in particular (and there are more of them than you think), really do need to recognise the historical aspect of the research. This may not matter if they simply want to have their trains running with readily purchased card buildings or a mix-match of rolling stock. However, I believe that for anyone who wants to achieve the correct atmosphere and accuracy, and present a layout, or even a piece of rolling stock, that authentically represents a particular prototype, he or she does need an insight into the relevant historical aspect.

The North British Railway

So I will look at the five main companies and it will come as no surprise that we start in North British Railway territory. That is not because it is my own particular interest, but because it eventually became the largest of the five companies in terms of track mileage operated. Biggest did not actually mean the best, or most profitable, as we shall see. For many years, particularly during the early years of its existence, the NBR was invariably in financial straits. Its use of old and outdated rolling stock caused the paying public to complain in the press and elsewhere on numerous occasions. It did eventually have an extensive route mileage in southern Scotland including its original line, which ran from Berwick to Edinburgh. This had the lucrative East Coast traffic from London, but the company even ran into bother with that when the North Eastern Railway managed to obtain running rights from Berwick into the capital, thus restricting the revenue earned by the NBR.

It also absorbed the Edinburgh and Glasgow Railway, which had the shortest route between the two cities. Numerous suburban lines and branches within the two major cities featured intensive

workings whilst further main lines extended northward, whereby NBR trains could, through running powers on other companies' lines, reach Aberdeen. The coalfields throughout the central belt of Scotland and in Fife also fell prey to the NBR whilst a further main line route, the Waverley Route, between Edinburgh and Carlisle was also absorbed shortly after its opening as far as Hawick. Further inroads were made in the Western Highlands to Fort William and Mallaig, fish and tourism being the main interest, whilst the company was also involved in the crossing of the mighty Firths of Tay and Forth.

It was also one of the few Scottish companies to have any considerable track mileage within England. This it did with the three lines in Northumberland as well as a line between Carlisle and Silloth. As an aside, it must have been glorious to be 'train spotting' at Carlisle just prior to 1923. There you could have witnessed not only the brown or bronze green NBR locomotives but also examples including the black London and North Western Railway engines, the crimson of the Midland, the green of the Glasgow and South Western Railway, the blue of the Caledonian Railway as well as locomo-

Left: a classic West Highland style signal box at Glenfinnan in 1983

Below: Rannoch station in 1976. The two-tone green colour scheme was applied at some time during the early 1970s. *(Photographs: the author)*

Centre: An unusual split-level station construction on the former North British main line at Markinch, seen in 1995. *(Photograph: Steve Flint)*

Bottom: designs for smaller stations in the Borders were markedly different from other parts of the North British system. Those at Deadwater (left) and Longwitton (right) survive as private residences. *(Photographs: the author)*

North British Railway House Style

The North British Railway was spread over a large geographical area and thus had a diverse style of architecture that corresponded with the various smaller companies it had absorbed. Perhaps the most distinctive was the West Highland chalet style seen above and right.

In the central region a more classical style could be found at places such as Markinch in Fife (centre) but generally smaller NBR stations would be served by less grandiose single storey brick, stone or timber buildings, such as Kilconquhar (page 50) and St Cyrus (page 71). A design used frequently on branches and suburban lines was that represented by my various models of Eyemouth (see Lochside opposite).

In the Borders Region, the style was different again, with mainly stone or timber single storey structures such a those seen at Deadwater and Longwitton (below, see also pages 9 and 15)

This diversity reinforces the need to research your chosen locality carefully, especially so if you want your layout to appear authentic and believable.

tives in the greens of the North Eastern Railway and the Maryport and Carlisle Railway. Add to that the fine array of coaching stock, and an extremely colourful view of the pre-grouping scene would be visible.

The NBR had some of the most robust and long lasting classes of locomotives in the country. They were quite handsome despite their strange pre-grouping colours, which could range from brown to bronze or olive green depending upon the lighting conditions! Most of the passenger locomotives were actually 4-4-0s and the company never built a six-coupled passenger locomotive or an eight-coupled freight locomotive. However, the last 0-6-0 to work in Scotland was an old NBR 'C' class 0-6-0 (J36) constructed during the late nineteenth century. Fortunately for modellers, some 4mm and 7mm kits have been produced of NBR prototypes. The NBR became part of the LNER in 1923.

The Caledonian Railway

The second largest company in terms of route mileage was the old rival of the NBR, the Caledonian Railway. This company actually had its origins in England, being closely connected with the London and North Western Railway. It was instrumental in reaching Carlisle and, seeing the growth of industry in Scotland and especially in and around Glasgow, decided to assist with the construction of a line over the border from Carlisle to Glasgow. Other companies at the time had the same idea but the LNWR managed to construct the line, which is now known as the West Coast Main Line. The company they helped to form was the Caledonian Railway, a name that gave the impression to the travelling public in Scotland, at least, that it intended to reach out to all parts of the country.

It too eventually absorbed numerous smaller concerns, gaining valuable access to mineral resources. The Caledonian invariably built double track main lines rather than the single track routes which other companies concentrated on. This showed to the public that it was really a very important company and added to its prestige. It also gave Scotland some of the best stretches of main line in the country. By a series of

Caledonian Railway House Style

Caledonian Railway signal boxes were quite distinctive with some different styles illustrated here. Each could be found at localities across the company's territory depending on period of construction or upgrading. The final Caledonian 'standard' design had large window panes and decorative cornices (centre).

Station styles were varied too, but one characteristic common to many stone-built Caledonian stations are the crow stepped gables, as seen below at Kirknewton.

Top right: Alloa Junc. box on the CR main line to Stirling, c. 1972. *(Photograph: Santona Publications Library)*

Centre: A classic CR box from Garnqueen South Junc., restored by the SRPS and preserved on the Bo'ness and Kinneil Railway. *(Photograph: the author)*

Below: the ex-CR station building at Kirknewton in 2006. *(Photograph: Steve Flint)*

amalgamations, it reached Stirling, Perth, Dundee and then Aberdeen. Edinburgh had been reached from Carstairs as well as by more minor routes in the central belt of Scotland. It extended its lines to the west coast towns of Ardrossan and built one of the finest stations in Scotland at Wemyss Bay. The Caledonian too, reached the West Highlands, although it took a number of years, finally reaching Oban via Callander and the Trossachs. It also inherited the docks at Grangemouth which are still active today. Within Glasgow and Edinburgh itself, two magnificent stations were created, Central

Station in Glasgow, which was greatly expanded in 1899, and Princes Street Station within Edinburgh. That fine terminus unfortunately closed in 1965.

The company built magnificent locomotives, many with outside cylinders and long boilers in the early days. It persuaded Dugald Drummond to leave the North British and he produced some of the best locomotives of his career for the Caledonian. Later on J.F. McIntosh introduced a number of sturdy yet beautiful locomotives, the most famous being perhaps his Cardean 4-6-0 class. At first Caledonian locomotives were

Dalmally Signal Box (ex-Caledonian)

Scale 4mm = 1ft (1:76)

0   5ft   10ft

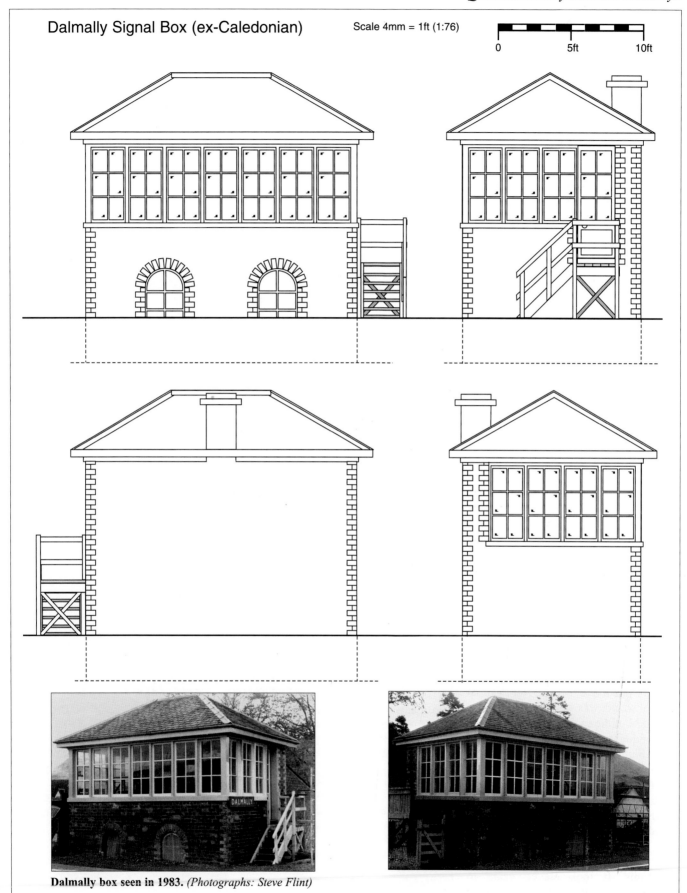

Dalmally box seen in 1983. *(Photographs: Steve Flint)*

painted dark blue and then later light blue. Again, many of its locomotives worked through into British Railways days and frequently looked well in the livery of that period.

From a modeller's point of view, the Caledonian is reasonably represented in kit form - and who can forget the Tri-ang version of the Caledonian Single No. 123 and its two coaches? Not quite representative of the day to day running perhaps, but an insight as to how well the Caledonian livery was portrayed. The Caledonian became part of the LMS at the grouping in 1923.

The Glasgow and South Western Railway
The third pre-grouping company within Scotland had a much more easily defined geographical area. The Glasgow and South Western more or less served the south western region of Scotland. It too had an impressive station in Glasgow, St Enoch, which also closed in the 1960s. However, its main locomotive works was at Kilmarnock and it was from here that many of its routes radiated from. The west coast resorts along the Ayrshire Coast along with Girvan saw plenty of traffic whilst the port of Stranraer was of importance with its ferries across to Ireland. Stranraer used to also be reached via the 'Port Road' route from Carlisle and Dumfries, which was actually a joint line with the Caledonian, but it too succumbed to closure in the 1960s. The G&SWR had its own main line from Carlisle to Glasgow, which was probably a slower route than the Caledonian line, but it is still operating today with some of the services into Scotland originating from Tyneside.

It was mineral wealth that enabled the G&SWR to prosper although it remained the poor relation to the end. Not all of its mineral wealth was within its territory. A great deal of the coal in particular, was to be found in transit through its territory to either South Wales or the Clyde ports. It was involved in constructing the City of Glasgow Union Railway, a line only six or so miles long. The line was built in order to tranship goods from the G&SWR to the Edinburgh and Glasgow lines and so avoid using the Caledonian lines and thus having to pay additional premiums. It took eleven years to construct, and for those modellers

interested in purely urban lines, it is indeed an interesting prototype worth further research.

Many of the locomotives built for the G&SWR were essentially freight locomotives but they had excellent pedigrees, as did the designers; Hugh Smellie, James Manson, Peter Drummond and

R. H. Whitelegg, to name but four. Passenger locomotives did not seem to make the impression with the public but were always equal to the task. Towards the end of the pre-grouping era, the G&SWR built six 4-6-4 or 'Baltic' tank locomotives. They were designed by Whitelegg and were possibly the most

Glasgow & South Western Railway House Style

Above and centre: the sectional timber station building design used by the G&SWR was distinctive and appeared at many smaller stations. This one at Fairlie on the Largs branch is pictured in the late 1960s. (see also page 45 and 46) *(Photographs: Stuart Rankin)*

Right: also very distinctive were the company's signal boxes. There were seven 'standard' designs, the later ones being fitted with large panes as seen on Kirkconnel box in 1984. The stove-pipe chimney is particularly characteristic of G&SWR boxes.
(Photograph: Ian Fleming)

powerful of all Scottish locomotives.

The Glasgow and South Western Railway seems to be rarely modelled in whatever scale, but some of its routes were extremely attractive. There were plenty of wayside stations and many of its branch lines were fascinating, especially if you enjoy short pick-up freight trains and two or three coach passenger workings. The area in the south of the region between Stranraer and Dumfries, has long-closed railway lines just waiting to be researched and modelled. The G&SWR became part of the LMS at the grouping

The Highland Railway
We now turn to the fourth company, the Highland Railway; its name conjures up

images of trains amongst remote beauty, mountains and lochs. The Highland did not have to contend with the luxury of building routes where it liked. Basically, it had to follow the geography of the land and as a result traversed some wild and desolate countryside. Its routes served the territory north of Perth and were invariably single track. It could be said that the Highland Railway was built in order to provide routes from all directions to the regional capital, Inverness. Here there were links to the far north towns of Wick and Thurso and west along the 'Skye Line' from Dingwall to the Kyle of Lochalsh and ferries to the Western Isles. The fledgling Highland Railway came about by the usual amalgamations of smaller local concerns,

and there was never much in the way of competition for it, except perhaps to the east of Inverness, where, amongst the rich coastal farm land and important fishing ports, relations with the Great North of Scotland Railway were not always friendly. That competition, however, did bring about the construction of many pretty branch lines by both the Highland and the Great North of Scotland, mainly to capture the fish and farming traffic in the land between Inverness and Aberdeen. Many of them warrant attention from interested modellers and it is surprising that so few layouts of this delightful and undiscovered backwater of railway charm are ever built. The Highland did of course have its own expensive main line between Inverness, Aviemore and Stanley Junction, just north of Perth itself. An earlier main line (of sorts) existed between Forres and Aviemore via Dava and Grantown on Spey. This was a rather circuitous route south, and despite passing through several centres of population, the Highland opened a more direct route to Aviemore via Carr Bridge in 1898. It was expensive to construct but, as usual, was a political move in order to keep the Great North of Scotland Railway at bay.

Fortunately, many of the Highland's lines remain in use to this day, mainly the key routes north and south. Modellers who travel these routes today can gain an insight into the hardships that the lines must have operated under. The weather can be fierce in Scotland but in the far north, it can be merciless, threatening yet extremely stunning all at the same time.

Left: in pre-grouping days, brown/red oxide for wooden structures and woodwork was used widely across Scotland; as above and here, on Peter Fletcher's Highland Railway layout, Ardbealach. The cream with brown framework scheme came in after the grouping and lasted into the 1960s when white appeared, with framework in blue, grey or black. *(Photograph: Steve Flint)*

Highland Railway House Style

Although several styles existed from the constituent companies which were absorbed by the Highland Railway, notably the Rosshire Extension and the Sutherland and Caithness on the Far North Line (see page 77), the Highland generally favoured an H-plan for both its masonry and timber station buildings as seen here.

Left: Brora station, an H-plan design in masonry, seen here in 1990. Similar structures can still be found on the Highland's southern main line to Perth.

Centre left: Carr Bridge, on the 1898 built direct, line seen in 1987. It shows the board and batten timber design, again in H-plan, that the Highland used at numerous localities from the 1890s.

Below: a shorter variation on the timber design - minus one wing, was used at smaller stations, such as Plockton seen here in 1975. *(Photographs: Steve Flint)*

Equally, many of the original wayside stations are still open, often still with the distinctive wooden station buildings, goods sheds (albeit turned over to another use) and signal boxes. Modernisation and refurbishment have resulted in one or two more modern structures appearing on the company's former routes, especially between Inverness and Aberdeen. The new station building at Keith for instance (though principally of GNoSR origin), is really quite attractive. It is of course still possible to trace many of the abandoned branch lines in the area because the earthworks are still in place.

Left: Helmsdale signal box in 1982. Board and batten cladding and a corrugated iron roof was typical of almost all Highland boxes. Smaller boxes often had four-pane window frames. *(Photograph: Steve Flint)*

The locomotives that worked the Highland lines were all interesting and well built with distinctive features that looked equally well in the plain Highland green, the red or crimson of the LMS, or indeed the more sombre black of the British Railways era. The LMS Black Five locomotives were the mainstay of the motive power after the Highland locomotives were withdrawn. Perhaps the most famous locomotive of that era was the 'Jones Goods' but many of the smaller locomotives, in particular the 4-4-0 types were easily identified by their bulbous outside cylinders. They worked the sometime harsh conditions on the Highland routes well for many decades.

Perhaps the most interesting appeal to modelling the Highland routes lies in the fact that at the end of the nineteenth century, and again in the 1920s, plans to build many new lines were considered, especially in the sparsely populated Western Highlands and more details about these proposals can be found on page 78. The Highland also looked at building lines on the Isle of Skye and Lewis, however, the most important line which the company planned, but never actually constructed, was the possible connection between Fort Augustus and Inverness. The plan was actually a revisit of part of an earlier scheme proposed as the Glasgow and North Western Railway in the 1880s: what a superb route through the Great Glen and along the shores of Loch Ness that would have made (see the panel on the G&NWR at the end of this chapter). At the Grouping in 1923, the Highland became part of the LMS.

The Great North of Scotland Railway
We can now conclude our look at the five pre-grouping companies by considering the smallest of them, the Great North of Scotland Railway. The area it covered was quite small, to the North and West of Aberdeen, across the old counties of Aberdeen, Banff and Moray. In the early days of the company, which was formed in 1845, the main intention was to link Aberdeen with Inverness. It is a well known fact, as recorded in the journals of the time, that it was a troublesome company to deal with. Its relations with the Caledonian at Aberdeen invariably stemmed from the fact the all the fish landed at Aberdeen and other surround-

ing harbours, which was considered by the GNoSR as its own traffic, usually had to be forwarded south via the Caledonian. Relationships in the west were possibly worse. It took the GNoSR so long to complete their own main line from Aberdeen that other local companies decided to build their own route into Inverness. For quite sometime the GNoSR had to hand over its services at Elgin; whilst it is possible it could have built its own route to Inverness (from its Speyside line to Boat of Garten), it naturally felt the Highland possibly had a hand in all of the goings on, and its

directors were probably right in their assumptions! It took the Railway and Canal Commissioners four years to finally sort out the feud in 1897.

The fishing harbours along the coastline between Inverness and Aberdeen saw the GNoSR construct a number of branch lines and frequently they were long single track affairs to places such as Lossiemouth, Portsoy, Banff and Macduff. Interestingly, the latter two terminus stations more or less faced each other across Banff Bay, though it was almost a one hundred mile round trip between the two by rail. Further along the

Great North of Scotland Railway House Style

Above: for a small company, the GNoSR had a remarkable variety of building styles and are worth further research in their own right. This one at Dufftown, seen in 1994, was typical of the masonry structures on the Speyside route and would fit well on any layout so located. *(Photographs: Steve Flint)*

Left: four general types of signal box are noted for the GNoSR, this example at Oldmeldrum is a 'Type 2b', seen in 1959. *(Photograph: I Dunbar, GNSRA)*

coast and down the east side were lines to Fraserburgh, St Combs, Peterhead and Cruden Bay, many with quaint junction stations placed seemingly in the middle of nowhere, but nevertheless delightful little locations crying out to be modelled. Not perhaps set amongst spectacular scenery such as those in other parts of Scotland, but ones which would make ideal projects particularly for modellers who prefer to build just up to the boundary fence.

The company pioneered the use of motor bus traffic to feed into its stations and commuter traffic was introduced between Dyce and Aberdeen. As Dyce is the location of Aberdeen Airport, services today have been increased to serve the needs of travellers and industry, with a half hourly service into the city. The route mileage of the company was very small at about three hundred miles and was mostly single track. There were few engineering difficulties, apart from some impressive bridges over the rivers in the area, and its motive power was quite distinctive in that it relied upon locomotives of the 4-4-0 design. It did build some 0-4-4 tank locomotives for the Aberdeen suburban services and some 0-4-2 tank locomotives for Aberdeen docks. Once the Great North of Scotland Railway became part of the LNER, many other classes worked the lines although two types of GNoSR 4-4-0s continued to work in British Railway days.

As with many other pre-grouping railway companies throughout the UK, railway modellers are not really too well served when it comes down to sourcing models relating to GNoSR prototypes. As we shall see, it is frequently a case of building kits, if they are available, or scratch building rolling stock for a pre-group layout, unless you are interested in the British Railways period, or the various diesel periods. If you are interested in the current scene, it's a case of obtaining some Class 158 DMUs for the passenger services and the freight can be handled with Class 66 and Class 67 diesels. All these models are available in 2mm and 4mm. There is of course the little matter of the Caledonian Sleeper trains to consider however!

Before drawing this chapter to a close, we must not overlook the fact that most of the pre-grouping companies also operated shipping services. Many of these were along the River Clyde in order to capture the lucrative traffic from wealthy Glasgow businessmen, who had their villas in the coastal resorts. Other railways were involved with the shipping routes to the Western Isles, although eventually David Macbrayne captured most of that traffic. As we shall see, the delights of incorporating a shipping or ferry activity adjacent to the station on the layout can be irresistible, and where else but in Scotland are there countless opportunities for such schemes?

There were tourist-based steamer services in the Trossachs and on Loch Lomond as well, and special trains would be run in connection with them. Many of these actually ran well into British Railways days and frequently this would bring the sight of first generation Diesel Multiple Units into areas which rarely witnessed them.

It is also worth remembering that the bus services in Scotland, especially in the Highlands, would frequently work closely with the railway companies so that buses were timetabled to meet trains. I recently saw this happen at Achnasheen on the Kyle line, so modellers do perhaps need a slight knowledge of bus transport too, irrespective of period. There are numerous photographs showing the attractive Macbrayne buses meeting trains at the old Fort William station. Today, they wait outside the station next to the Morrisons Supermarket.

That really concludes this brief outline of the five pre-grouping companies, as I said at the beginning of this chapter, it is not a comprehensive historical treatise, that would be out of place in this book which is about modelling and layout building. If you would like to find out more about the history of Scotland's Railways before building your layout then see the appendix 'Further Research'.

Finally, before moving on, take a look at the panel below about the proposed Glasgow and North Western Railway: the most spectacular railway proposal in the UK, in my opinion.

The Glasgow and North Western Railway Proposal

Not long after the Oban line had opened in 1880, a new line was proposed from Glasgow as a direct route to Inverness. It was called the Glasgow and North Western Railway and it was to run by Loch Lomond and Glen Falloch to Crianlarich, where there was already a station on the Oban line. From here it was to traverse the edge of Rannoch Moor, heading north west to Kingshouse at the head of Glencoe. Then it would then descend due west through Glencoe, cross the narrows at the mouth of Loch Leven and arrive at the shore of Loch Linnhe. Here it would turn north by north east and head to Fort William.

From here the route would have been through Glen Lochy and into the Great Glen, whence it would follow the shores of Loch Ness to its target destination of Inverness.

A grandiose scheme through some of Scotland's most majestic scenery: but loud alarm bells rang within the Caledonian and Highland Railway camps and eventually in 1883, the bill failed. The G&NWR proposal leaves us with dreams of what might have been and although the route of the present day A82 follows closely the intended railway route, driving in a car is no substitute for relaxing by a window seat in an old BR Mk1. A map of the proposed G&NWR route is shown below, whilst opposite, I present a just supposing layout scheme set on the shores of Loch Ness in the Great Glen.

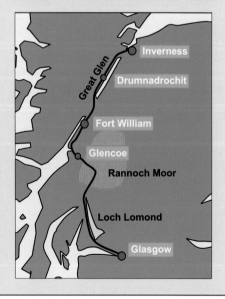

DRUMNADROCHIT

If I am honest, apart from the outstanding location at Loch Ness, surrounded by mountainous and forested scenery, this project owes more to its name than anything else. Just imagine, one of those BR light blue station nameboards, adorning a small wayside station, with this romantic Scottish name. I have driven through this location frequently and have just supposed that a line had eventually reached Inverness from Fort William through the Great Glen. Perhaps as a result of the G&NWR proposal, or even a later proposal. Either way it would have made my layout 'Loch Lochy' a through station, probably in the same location as Gairloch had been, on the ill-fated Spean Bridge to Fort Augustus line. A line from Fort Augustus up the glen would have invariably followed the north western shore of Loch Ness because that is where most of the small settlements are.

There is really only one main road (A82), and that follows the suggested route closely. Drumnadrochit is about 15 miles from Inverness and the village itself is located on a sort of horseshoe, which leads into Glen Urquhart. Standing on a promontory at the entrance to the Glen and overlooking Loch Ness is Urquhart Castle, a local tourist attraction nowadays. Whether the railway line followed the road into the village and then rejoined Loch Ness on the other side of the river, is matter for conjecture. I would like to think it ran across where the river actually entered Loch Ness, but perhaps that would have been an expensive structure to build. In any case, the river has to be crossed, so somewhere on the layout, will be a bridge. Perhaps the platforms ran out onto the bridge like at Hawick, always an interesting scenic item. No doubt the line would have been single track, but Drumnadrochit would have warranted a crossing loop and small goods yard. It may have followed the typical West Highland station style, and been an island platform, though I have suggested it would have had two facing platforms, as per the Mallaig line, but with one jutting out onto the bridge.

If set during the 1970s, the ubiquitous but typical Sulzer roar of the Class 26s and 27s would have been heard echoing across Loch Ness as they plied their three or four coaches on this leisurely and picturesque journey.

Much of the freight by this time would have been through freights between Inverness and Fort William. Aluminium related traffic could have run via this much shorter route between the smelters at Fort William and Invergordon. Pipes could be sent that way for use by the oil and gas industry. Timber traffic could originate at Drumnadrochit itself, as well as further north, which along with pulp, could be run to Corpach. Outward paper products could travel to north east Scotland.

Permanent Way traffic would also exist and use the sidings. Thus plenty of opportunities exist to operate modest sized freight trains or mixed passenger and parcels services too.

The layout could be built with twin fiddle yards at either end, or for a permanent location, into an oval around a room perimeter. The lochside scenery could be extended around the curves making this project, with its interesting traffic patterns and scenic splendour, a very attractive proposition, steam or diesel, to suit your preferred period.

Drumnadrochit at a glance

Design scale: 4mm. **Suggested period:** 1970s. **Location:** Loch Ness. **Locomotive types:** Various Type 2 classes. **Typical traffic:** passenger trains on Fort William - Inverness services, oil, timber, paper products in vans or sheeted opens, aluminium related traffic.

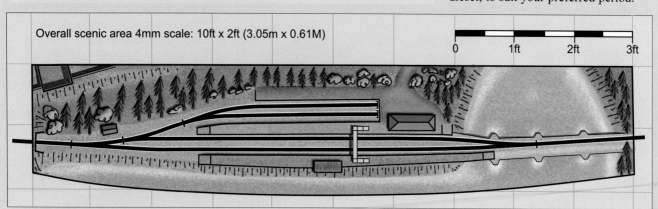

Overall scenic area 4mm scale: 10ft x 2ft (3.05m x 0.61M)

0   1ft   2ft   3ft

Chapter 3
In Border Country

The 'Border Country' is perhaps the area I identify most with, it being close to my native Tyneside and the source of much inspiration for my layout building over the years. Other authors have described the Border Region extending into south west Scotland, but for me, it has to be the area running either side of the present day border itself; between a point just north of Carlisle to a point just north of Berwick upon Tweed. Another, perhaps easier way to describe this most attractive region from a railway point of view, is to look at the main line between Carlisle and Edinburgh - the famed Waverley Route - and consider it, and the many branch lines that radiated from it as: The Railways of Border Country.

Sadly the Waverley Route closed in January 1969, a sadness that was further compounded for me personally by the fact that I was completing my final teaching practice in Hawick during the spring of 1971 when the line was being dismantled: all I saw during that period was a solitary 08 diesel shunter hauling spoil trains into Hawick yard. Most, if not all of its associated branch lines had been systematically closed prior to that January 1969 date, and indeed there was the feeling, at least in the Borders, that the freight services operating over the route latterly were deliberately moved onto other routes. The line actually handled more freight during its last years of operation than at any time during its hundred-plus years of existence!

Historically, the Borders area had been fought over for many years: even today ceremonies are carried out in reverence of the Border feuds and it proved to be no different when the first railways were projected between England and Scotland.

Naturally, most of the branch lines were originally local concerns, but the territory between Edinburgh and Carlisle was hotly disputed, between the Caledonian Railway and its ally the London and North Western Railway, and their joint enemy: the North British Railway. Eventually, the company gained the authorisation

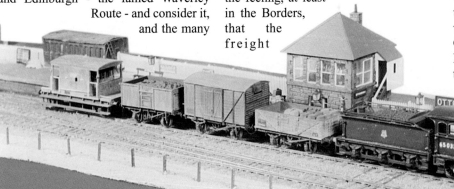
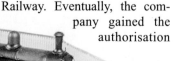

Left: my Otterburn schemes were based on a supposed branch off the Wansbeck Valley line at Woodburn. My recent 7mm version is seen, top, with an ex-NER J21 No. 65042 arriving. The original 4mm version from 1979 (below) shows another J21 on goods.
(Photographs: the author)

Right: The Waverley Route epitomised by this scene on the Riddings Junction layout built by Eddie Ford and the Birtley Club.
(Photograph: Steve Flint)

to build a line south to Hawick and then extend it over the border into Carlisle. Even after gaining authorisation, the line had to be constructed through some of the most difficult countryside in southern Scotland, resulting in treacherous gradients and curves. The company's problems did not go away after completion of the route in July 1862, as the line itself was starved of traffic by the Caledonian and LNWR until the Midland Railway opened its Settle and Carlisle route from Leeds in 1876. The NBR then had a willing partner to work with.

Carlisle Citadel station was the starting point for NBR trains to commence a journey north to Edinburgh over the Waverley Route. In order to gain access into the station the NBR absorbed and operated a small line to Port Carlisle. It also leased a line in 1862 to Silloth Docks, which it felt would give it a means of sending freight southwards as well as to Ireland. The NBR even operated a small shipping fleet serving Belfast, Dublin and Liverpool. In the pre-grouping period, the LNWR and Caledonian made other companies pay 'track charges' to enter Carlisle Citadel. The Port Carlisle line closed in 1932 and an interesting route from that line crossed the Solway Firth over a viaduct between Bowness-on-Solway and Kirtlebridge in Scotland. This allowed traffic to bypass Carlisle until the viaduct closed in 1921. I believe the very nature of the shifting sands in the Solway Firth contributed to its demise.

Silloth was quite a spacious station with many sidings for the huge traffic the line generated in freight. There were weekend passenger specials in order to allow the people of Carlisle to have a day at the seaside. However, after World War Two, much of this traffic was lost as road transport took its grip of the movement of goods. Like many lines, it managed to

struggle on until December 1964, a period in history when many lines were closed. Despite by then being under LMR control, the Scottish 'connection' survived, with Haymarket Class 26s being seen in charge of trains on the branch. Heading northwards, the first proper branch (if you ignore a small branch to Gretna which closed in 1915) was to Langholm. This was a 7 mile single track line from Riddings Junction to Langholm, opened in 1864. Originally the Caledonian had proposed a line through Langholm although in the end, the NBR built the short branch after bypassing the town with its Waverley Route. The line closed to passenger services in 1964 and freight lasted until 1967. The terminus at Langholm offers potential for modelling. Although larger than

my preferred three or four point approach, it is an attractive candidate for a historical modelling treatise.

Riddings Junction has been modelled on at least two occasions, once in 4mm (above) by Eddie Ford and members of the Birtley Club in County Durham, and more recently in N gauge by Steve Fairlie of the East Neuk MRC. It is an interesting 'country junction' station with an island platform which the Langholm branch train used, with extensive services operating on the main line.

After Riddings Junction, the Waverley route climbed across the border, through the small town of Newcastleton, into the rolling hills past Steele Road and then arrived at a station of sheer isolation: Riccarton Junction. The nearest public road was two miles

Left: country junctions always make modelling favourites and Reedsmouth, with its unusual end-on signal box, is no exception. Here, the Wansbeck Valley Line branched off the Border Counties route and is pictured in the 1950s with a J21 running around an excursion train.
(Photograph: R. Paine/R. W. Lynn Collection)

away, and I know by experience as I have walked to the site many times; the easiest way to get there is to follow the old Border Counties line from the direction of Saughtree. Riccarton Junction was built to form an interchange between the two routes, which both opened on the same day in 1862. A locomotive depot, and even a Co-op on the platform, were provided, but it must have been an isolated life for the hundred or so souls who lived and worked there. Older children were taken to Hawick for schooling, although a small primary school was eventually built in Riccarton itself. Special train arrangements were made for church services, although I think such services were even conducted in the station building from time to time!

However, I must now digress away from the Waverley route and take a look along the routes that have held a special interest for me since childhood. First of course, is the Border Counties Railway. From Riccarton Junction this line was built down the North Tyne valley through Kielder and Bellingham, and the delightful Reedsmouth Junction with its unusual end-on signal box, to Hexham on the NER's Newcastle-Carlisle line. Eastwards from Reedsmouth Junction, the Wansbeck Valley Railway opened a

Border Counties Structures

The station building on Otterburn was based upon the structure at Woodburn (right) and was constructed with a plywood frame covered with embossed plastic stone sheet. The roof consisted of cartridge paper strips with notched cut-outs to create individual tiles. Chimney stacks were fabricated from balsa wood with chimney pots made from off-cuts of plastic sprue. Window frame bars are strips cut from white sticky labels and pressed onto clear plastic glazing. The stone sheet was weathered heavily using matt black paint, which was then wiped off with a tissue. The signal cabin is based on the typical Border Counties style found at several locations, of which Woodburn is one example.
(Photographs: right, R. W. Lynn; below, the author)

Angerton Station

This little station on the Wansbeck Valley line has always been a favourite of mine. The two shots above show the station shortly before closure; left, a 12T van can be seen at the small loading dock, whilst, right, the loop and sidings appear to be out of use. The colour shot after closure (right) shows an ex-NBR coach in use as a platform store. These became a feature of many small stations on ex-NBR lines, as will be seen in many shots throughout this book. *(Photographs: author's collection).*

cross-country branch in stages across Mid-Northumberland, eventually providing a route from Reedsmouth to Morpeth on the East Coast Main Line. It was from this point, the NBR had attempted to run services into Newcastle via the Blyth and Tyne system, however the Blyth and Tyne Railway was eventually purchased by the North Eastern Railway and thoughts of a NBR through line to Newcastle diminished, although they did seek operating rights from Hexham into Newcastle. An even smaller concern, the Northumberland Central Railway, operated a branch from midway on the Wansbeck line at Scotsgap Junction, to Rothbury. Originally, this line was intended to have been much larger and was to have gone further north to reach Coldstream, just over the Border. It never got there, but that historical proposal

allows us to use our modeller's license and conjure up might-have-been stations, maybe amongst the Cheviot Hills, an area which even in the 21st century is still remote and beautiful, or across the Millfield Plain area to Ford near the border (see my proposed scheme to Ford Castle on page 35).

Incidentally, it was during the late 1970s when I lived in Tyneside that I first became interested in matters North British. Myself, along with two like minded souls, Richard Heard and Paul Rhodes: all three of us teachers as it happens, would frequently head up into mid-Northumberland to explore the Wansbeck and Rothbury Lines. These lines have provided lots of inspiration for my layouts, including my Otterburn schemes, the buildings on my 7mm version being similar in style to those at

Woodburn (see panel opposite). Another delightful station that the three of us were equally captivated by was Angerton, although it had been closed for ten or more years when we came across it, the main structures were still in position and we did much measuring up of the site. This station would make an excellent introductory project into the finer 4mm scales and thus, I have no hesitation in including it has a detailed scheme in this book (above and overleaf).

Back on the Border Counties route, it was a small coalfield at Plashetts that had been the main reason for building the Border Counties line although the seams were soon worked out, and the coal was found to be unsuitable for its intended market - the woollen mills of the Borders. Just supposing that the coalfield had been much larger though, and already we have

Angerton Station Buildings

Scale 2mm = 1ft (1:152)

0   10ft   20ft

Right: by 1966 Angerton station, long closed to passengers, witnessed the passage of an occasional freight train. Here an ex-NER Class J27 No. 65860 is seen along-side the platform en-route to Woodburn. *(Photograph: L. Sadler)*

a scenario for the line to remain open for much longer. Mineral traffics have provided reasons for many isolated lines to survive, and perhaps this could even extend into the 1960s or 1970s with Class 24s and 37s on rakes of 21T coal hoppers, and green or blue 2 car DMUs on passenger services.

In truth however, these three lines in Northumberland soon became simply rural backwaters and eventually passenger services were withdrawn from the Wansbeck and Rothbury line in September 1952. The Border Counties succumbed in 1956, mainly because of

ANGERTON

The Wansbeck line was opened between Morpeth and Reedsmouth in stages between 1862 and 1865 and from looking at First and Second Edition 25ins Ordnance Survey maps, it is obvious that changes were made to the stations, probably during the mid 1890s. Angerton station was practically midway between Morpeth and Scotsgap and was a charming location.

The line was on a gentle curve and entered the station from the Morpeth direction through a cutting. There was a single platform, a small goods yard with loading facilities on the loop, as well as a very short end loading siding close to the level crossing. This short siding could only accommodate about one wagon and there was a wooden sleeper style hut close to the entrance to the yard. By this shed was a small coal-weighing machine. Immediately after the level crossing, which had two gates, the loop ended and the line dropped away on a slight embankment before crossing the River Wansbeck.

The area surrounding the station was a mixture of arable and cattle grazing land, although horse traffic was apparently quite common at the station, especially from Ireland. Behind the station building was a small wood and the road leading onto the level crossing curved away through it. The fine sandstone station building incorporated the station-masters dwelling as well as the usual facilities. The platform was quite low, at under three feet, but that was not at all unusual at some NBR stations. At the Morpeth end was a corrugated iron hut which was possibly an oil or lamp store. There were two further structures on the platform; a wooden planked shed containing a nine lever ground frame, and an old NBR grounded coach body, which would have been used as a store. As luck would have it, Richard Heard took a coloured photograph of these two structures.

I actually built the station in 4mm P4, and Richard did too. My model lives on, disguised as an LNWR branch and residing in the Home Counties I think. It consisted of the station as a scenic section with two small hidden

sidings, turntable style, at each end. Being quite a compact layout, I would recommend this approach, although it would be easy to build it as a continuous run, with a ladder of storage sidings at the back. In any case, you will get away with just two or three sidings because of the traffic patterns.

In September 1952, passenger services were curtailed. These had invariably consisted of an ex-NER G5 0-4-4T locomotive and one non-corridor brake third coach. It was sometimes strengthened with two extra coaches on Saturdays or market days. Angerton trains ran between Morpeth and Rothbury via Scotsgap Junction (a separate service existed between Scotsgap and Reedsmouth Junctions). The daily goods ran to a similar pattern and by the 1950s, J21s and J25s from North Blyth shed worked this meagre service. On Rothbury or Scotsgap market days, or indeed Rothbury race days, passenger traffic could be very heavy by comparison. Heavier J27 0-6-0s worked the two or three times a week freight services towards the end of the line's existence. This came in 1968, although Angerton station itself closed on the 3rd May 1964.

I suggested in the main text that this scheme would suit 4mm scale, a G5 tank and a J21 0-6-0, one brake third coach and half a dozen or so wagons is all that would be required, plus a non-fitted LNER or BR style brake van. Thus, even in 7mm scale it would be readily achievable, indeed it was the inspiration for me to commence 7mm scale modelling. From known traffic patterns, some specialist rolling stock would be required, especially horse-boxes and cattle wagons, agricultural machinery would arrive on Lowmacs, whilst hay traffic would require sheeted wagons. In the early days there had been quite an amount of mineral traffic, and even in later days, it has been estimated that two or three wagon-loads of domestic coal were off loaded at the station, all by hand apparently. So if you enjoy constructing specialist wagons, this would overcome the slight operating deficiencies the project has.

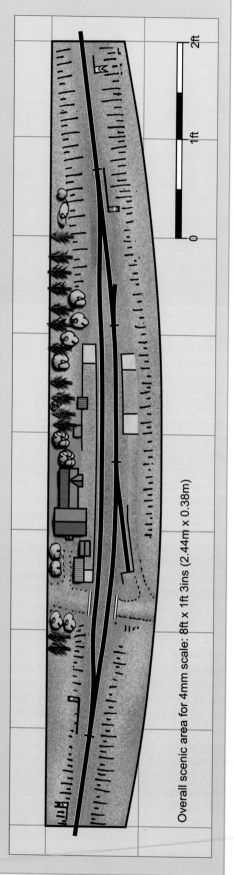

Overall scenic area for 4mm scale: 8ft x 1ft 3ins (2.44m x 0.38m)

Above: had the North British Railway built a line into Newcastle, they might have located their own terminus at Percy Street which I created in 0 Gauge during the 1990s as another 'just supposing' project. *(Photograph: the author.)*

the weak state of the bridge over the River Tyne at Border Counties Junction. Freight lingered on until 1966 along the Wansbeck line from Morpeth.

There were of course many other railway proposals across rural Northumberland and invariably the NBR had an interest in them. There were proposed branches to Belsay and Stamfordham, as well as the previously mentioned Ford. Interestingly enough, the proposed line through Belsay was to link into Scotsgap Junction as was the line to Stamfordham. Both these lines would have commenced in Newcastle with a proposed North British terminus station located in Percy Street, in the north of the city. Thus my trilogy of layouts, which included a 4mm terminus called 'Newcastle Haymarket' and the later 7mm layouts named 'Newcastle NB' and 'Percy Street' could have actually existed. If such a terminus had actually been built with some, or even all of the routes proposed, the NBR would have succeeded in its aim of having its own routes into the city. Whether any would have lingered on into British Railways days is doubtful, now that all services in the area use Newcastle Central station, but there are plenty of prototypes up and down the country where large cities still have more than one station.

Returning to the Waverley route, we now go to St Boswells where two branch lines linked the Waverley with the East Coast Main Line. One line from St

Boswells joined an earlier NER line at Kelso. This through route to Tweedmouth opened in 1851 and was mainly built to serve the rich agricultural land along the Tweed Valley. Kelso was the main station on the route, although Coldstream was an important junction station where the NER Wooler branch from Alnwick joined the Tweedmouth line. This NER branch was built to serve another agricultural region, but in reality it was to stop the NBR gaining a foothold in the area: remember the Rothbury branch was originally going to extend through this area and the residents were worried all the freight would have been siphoned off into the NBR lines.

Still within NBR territory on the St Boswells to Tweedmouth line (the NER owned the rest of the route from Sprouston) was that to the picturesque terminus at Jedburgh. This left the line at Roxburgh Junction: another appealing country junction set amongst rolling hills, although a little softer than those found around Riccarton, and despite its remoteness, the site was quite large and would demand a big area of baseboards for an authentic layout. At Jedburgh the station was laid out in a standard branch terminus format and even had its own locomotive shed. Jedburgh lost its passenger services in August 1948 because of the great floods of the time, which even blocked the East Coast Main Line. Freight was eventually restored and even an LMS Jubilee (No. 45696 *Arethusa*)

was recorded on the service in 1964. Like many of the adjacent lines, it closed in 1964. Passenger traffic on the Tweedmouth line also closed that year with freight finishing in two phases; 1965 and 1968.

The other route from St Boswells was slightly further to the north and entirely North British throughout. It passed through Greenlaw and Duns to join the East Coast Main Line at Reston. Constructed in two parts, the short stretch between Reston and Duns opened in 1849, whilst the remainder to St Boswells opened throughout in 1865. A beautiful viaduct over the River Tweed at Leaderfoot still stands today. Again, agriculture was the main aim of the line. The passenger services worked as two lines, St Boswells to Duns and Duns to Reston. Once again the floods of 1948 split the line into two when a bridge was washed away east of Greenlaw. The line never reopened as a through route. The Duns to Greenlaw passenger service lasted for another three years, closing in 1951 whilst the other longer section, from St Boswells to Greenlaw, never reopened to passenger traffic. Again, the freight traffic was lost to both lines between 1965 and 1966.

FORD CASTLE

As outlined in the main text, in the 1860s/80s there were a number of proposals to take a line through the centre of Northumberland up to the Scottish border, and in particular, the Kelso area. The main thrust was to utilise the Northumberland Central Railway, which had opened from Scotsgap to Rothbury. It was actually authorised to go beyond Rothbury and head over to the Millfield Plain, a very rich agricultural region more associated with the county town of Alnwick. The farming community would have preferred to send their wares to Alnwick and opposed the NCR scheme hoping the North Eastern Railway would help them out, which they eventually did.

In the event the NCR, like many rural schemes ran out of money and they had to seek permission to abandon the northern section. However, the original documentation indicated that the Scotsgap line was to 'end in the parish of Ford' and a branch would then be built from Ford to Cornhill on the NER Berwickshire branch. This would seem to indicate a terminal station near to the village of Ford, which also had a castle close by, hence the name 'Ford Castle'. None of this of course came to be, but I have always had in the back of my mind, a country junction scheme, based upon the station at Alnwick, which did indeed serve the area. Alnwick NER station was a grand

affair, mainly because the town is the seat of the Duke of Northumberland. Trains ran from the ECML at Alnmouth over a double-tracked branch the three or so miles to the terminus. Later on, the Cornhill Branch, as it was known, left Alnwick and headed northwards to Coldstream on the Berwickshire branch between Kelso and Tweedmouth.

At Alnwick the tracks ran past a tall signal box and then divided. Here in between the two tracks was a turntable. I have always thought this was an interesting use of space and just such an arrangement is suggested for 'Ford Castle', along with some exchange sidings like those at Reedsmouth. There is a small locomotive depot and enough platform faces to allow at least two different services to work into the station. I would envisage trains running from Scotsgap or Morpeth to Ford, although a better scheme might be to imagine a line built from Percy Street in Newcastle to Scotsgap, creating a through route to Scotland. Followers of my Newcastle trilogy of layouts will recognise the history of all this.

A further service would have linked Ford with Kelso or even Hawick, and this would have required its own platforms if connections were to be made with Newcastle. Yet another service may have been an express between Newcastle and Edinburgh, stopping only at Scotsgap, Ford Castle, Kelso,

Hawick and other main stations northwards on the Waverley Route. There would have been local pick-up freights as well as through freights to Tyneside, from Edinburgh and Glasgow.

I can imagine the Yorkshire Tankies (C15s) on the local Kelso to Ford service, with perhaps 'Scott' class locomotives hauling the through services to Edinburgh as well as the more local services from Newcastle. Pilot duties at Ford would utilise the lovely Holmes 'C' 0-6-0s (J36), whilst the larger Reid 'S' and 'B' 0-6-0s would handle the through freights. Bring the layout into the 1950s and the Scott 4-4-0s would still be hauling the passenger services with perhaps a D49 and K1 assisting, and the freight in the hands of say LNER B1s and K3s. Ex-NER locomotives would have infiltrated the rosters with J21 and J27 0-6-0s and perhaps a G5 on the passenger turns, whilst handsome V1 and V3 2-6-2Ts would have been seen too. It would be a long-term project, in any scale, as many of the locomotives required would need to be built up from kits. The only main problem I see would be the provision of NBR coaching stock. Some of the NBR bogie stock remained on the Border branches during the 1950s.

The turntable would be a 50ft type: large enough to turn the 'Scott' class locomotives although later types of motive power might have to work tender first. Overall an interesting project included because of its association with the Northumbrian branches as built. If a little more capital had been forthcoming in the 1860s, it may have actually existed and would not have come under the category of 'just supposing'!

Ford Castle at a glance

Design scale: 4mm. **Period:** 1920s LNER or 1950s BR. **Location:** North Northumberland, close to the Scottish Border. **Locomotive types:** see text. **Typical traffic:** cross-country passenger trains, freight; agricultural, cattle, coal, minerals, etc.

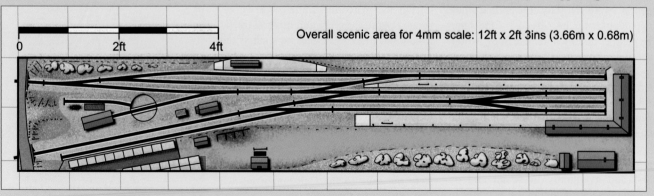

0   2ft   4ft

Overall scenic area for 4mm scale: 12ft x 2ft 3ins (3.66m x 0.68m)

Returning yet again to the Waverley route, there was a short six mile branch from Galashiels to Selkirk. This small town had numerous woollen mills as well as a wide agricultural area to serve but the passenger services were lost in 1951 with the eventual ending of freight in 1964. An interesting point about this branch, and one or two other branch lines in the Borders, was the use by the LNER of steam railcars in order to cut costs and because of the low number of passengers carried. Models of such prototypes are available in at least 4mm and 7mm scale, making them ideal passenger stock for a minimum space style of layout aimed at replicating the atmosphere of a rural Border branchline. There is even written evidence of them reaching Rothbury on excursions from Newcastle.

Continuing northwards along the Waverley Route to Fountainhall finds a little branch line constructed after the Light Railways Act had been passed at the very dawn of the twentieth century: the Lauder Light Railway, which opened in 1901. The act provided the means to build railways into areas which would benefit from such transport links but without the need for main line trackwork. As a consequence, motive power on the branch, which had a delightfully simple terminus, was restricted. In later days, some ex-Great Eastern tank locomotives, classification J69, operated the freight trains, and one at least, No. 68511, was recorded hauling an ex-NBR J36 tender behind it - now there's a prototype scenario that some would not believe. Passenger traffic ceased as long ago as 1932, but the freight service remained until 1958.

Peebles is another fine border town renowned for its spa. When the Waverley Route was proposed, the townsfolk of Peebles were slightly upset that their town would not be served by the main line. Little did they realise they would eventually be served by two companies, the NBR and the Caledonian. However, at first, they decided to build their own line from Eskbank, just south of Edinburgh, on the Waverley route which reached Peebles in 1855. A further branch was built from Leadburn, on the Peebles branch, to Dolphinton which opened in 1864 and eventually made an end on junction with Caledonian Railway line to

Dolphinton from Carstairs Junction in 1867. The Caledonian also built a line into Peebles from their station at Symington on the West Coast route in 1864 and eventually a short spur, which cut through the NBR goods yard, joined the two branches and was used mainly for the transfer of freight. However, there was precious little interaction between the Caledonian and the NBR, and consequently the NBR extended its own line south from Peebles to a junction on the Waverley route just north of Galashiels. This secured a route south from Peebles, opening late in 1864, with the lines becoming known as the Peebles Loop.

Despite such optimism in the mid-nineteenth century, the closure of the Peebles Loop and its associated branch lines began as early as 1933 when the Dolphinton passenger services were reduced (with freight going in 1960). The Caledonian station at Peebles closed in 1950, with the freight being withdrawn over a period of time until final closure in 1966. An early form of rationalisation was carried out on the Peebles Loop in the 1950s, with the introduction of some of the Modernisation Plan DMUs. Alas, the lines succumbed to closure in 1962, which just left the main Waverley route open. As we know, this too was slowly starved of traffic, despite there being plenty of new freight traffic including the car trains between Scotland and England.

At the Northern extremes of the Waverley Route, there were further branches off to the settlements at Penicuik, Polton and Glencourse. They served paper mills and gasworks as well as numerous coal mines in the East Lothian region. Any modellers wishing to construct a layout with intensive mineral traffic need look no further than this part of the Waverley Route.

On the Waverley route as a whole, steam operated freight and mineral traffic lasted into the 1960s. Classes such as the LMS Black Fives and the LNER B1s and V2s were the mainstay of the through freights. Some of the LNER Pacifics finished their working lives on the Waverley: my own particular favourite

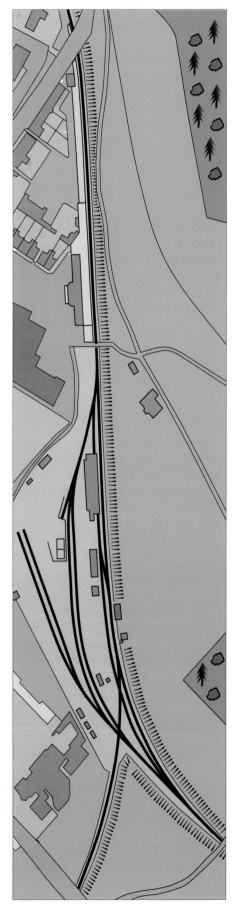

Right: the North British facilities at Peebles occupy a narrow enough site to be adapted into an L-shaped 'shelf' layout. Note the spur to the Caledonian branch that cuts across the goods sidings.

A3, 60041 'Salmon Trout', was a regular performer on Edinburgh and Carlisle services.

Modellers who enjoy the 'green' diesel period can also find much variety; in fact, the 1969 closure date allows for a significant Rail Blue presence too. Many of the larger diesels, often from LMR, NER and even WR depots, operated through freights; Classes 37, 40, 45, 46 and 47 were mostly involved, with the 45s also usually in charge of the through expresses to St Pancras. Even Class 50s and Deltics appeared on occasions, and not just on special workings.

Scottish-allocated Classes 24, 25 and 26 were commonplace on both freight and passenger traffic, although 27s were never allocated to Haymarket depot in great numbers and were consequently rarer. 20s were also scarce but the ill-conceived Class 17s were seen, frequently double-headed. Although fabled for their ability to catch fire, the pairing was probably as much to produce a useful amount of horsepower as for safety reasons!

As for the freight traffic itself, as well as the traditional 'mixed goods' there were also examples of the then-emerging 'block train' culture; for example the car trains mentioned earlier, and oil products, also being noted.

There are a number of other branch lines which radiated from Edinburgh and could possibly be linked to the Borders, although not directly connected to the Waverley Route. Again, most of these had their origins with the NBR although the Caledonian did reach a couple of locations within the Edinburgh area. Branch lines left the East Coast Main Line to Gullane, Macmerry, Haddington and Gifford. Some were quite modest stations and are quite easily modelled but they have all long since closed. The only survivor is the North Berwick branch. It had a fine terminus station, as befitted a seaside resort, but is now reduced to a basic 'long siding' with the original architecture swept away. For many years an outpost of first generation DMUs, it was electrified when the East Coast Main Line was converted in the 1980s. Since then a variety of EMUs have operated the services into Edinburgh Waverley although latterly a Class 90 and Mark 3 coaches have worked push-pull style. Strangely enough, it is proposed to use modern DMUs on the line although there is a problem with them being too long for the surviving platform!

I cannot conclude the Border Country section of book without reference to a particular favourite branch terminus of mine; the short two mile line from Burnmouth on the East Coast Main Line to the fishing port of Eyemouth. This line opened in 1891 simply to allow the fish catches to be transported to markets all over the country, and particularly along the East Coast and to London. It had the most simplistic track layout, four tracks fanning out with one track used for the

Left: an undated shot across the goods yard at Gullane. Passenger services ended in 1932 but freight lingered on until 1964. *(Photograph: WFRM collection)*

Below: The terminus at Haddington seen in 1943. Freight survived until 1968, just long enough to see Clayton Class 17s on occasional visits. *(Photograph: R. W. Lynn Collection)*

passenger traffic and end loading of fish. There was a siding, which dealt with the incoming coal traffic and then two further sidings alongside the Eye Water for the storage of vans. As I outline in more detail in the adjacent panel on Eyemouth, the release crossover in the station was removed and trains were subsequently shunted by gravity. In the 1950s, the one coach passenger service, complete with a J39, frequently had fish vans added to the rear of the train and these were shunted onto mainline services on arrival at Burnmouth. The branch was never dieselised, and whilst modeller's licence might allow it, I think the charm of this branch demands its recreation as a historical biography, and thus dieselisation

would be inappropriate. One day, I will model this attractive branch I feel sure, though devising a means of braking the train as it rolls back into the platform will be a challenging proposition.

With an interesting main line to consider, as well as lots of rural cross-country lines and branch termini, the borders provides a vast array of attractive modelling potential. Notwithstanding the 'just supposing' approach, it was a difficult choice to decide which prototype stations to present as suitable examples of the area and possible layout schemes in their own right. Always bearing in mind that most modellers are restricted for space and have financial constraints, I opted for smaller schemes. Later on, for devotees

of main line running, I will consider a rural station on the Waverley Route itself.

And finally, what happened to the three teachers who plotted and planned those models of Angerton? Well, one escaped to rural Norfolk via Warwickshire to become a Headteacher, Paul is a Headteacher in Oxfordshire and still modelling NER/NBR, and, as it happens, is an exceptional Northumbrian piper. Richard alone remained on Tyneside, also becoming a Headteacher, but nowadays pottering around in 7mm scale. What is quite unique, is that we are still in regular contact with each other, and we all enjoy the merits and delights of the North British Railway, especially within Northumberland.

Right: a busy little scene at Eyemouth in 1959 sees the sidings crammed with vans for fish traffic. J39 No. 64843 awaits to depart with the service for Burnmouth.
(Photograph: W. A. C. Smith)

Below: the tight release crossover can just be seen in this archive 1920s post-grouping shot of a branch passenger arrival.
(Photograph: author's collection)

EYEMOUTH

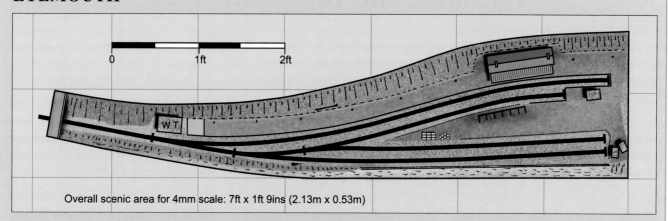

Overall scenic area for 4mm scale: 7ft x 1ft 9ins (2.13m x 0.53m)

This east coast branch line was but three miles in length and was originally built to haul fish from the harbour at Eyemouth. It is a particular favourite location of mine, and if modelled after the Grouping, only had three turnouts! Strange to relate, it is possible to model this line in the three major scales as rolling stock is available in 2mm, 4mm and 7mm. If you model the line during the last ten years of its existence, you would practically only require a J39 and a brake composite non-corridor coach along with a selection of fish vans and a few other freight vehicles.

The line was opened in 1891 and was operated by the NBR at the outset. It ran from sea level to a junction at Burnmouth on the East Coast Main Line. The intensive branch service operated with one locomotive on both passenger and freight workings. During the NB period, there was a release crossover between the platform road and the coal siding allowing the locomotive to run round its train, usually four or six-wheeled coaches. Much of the fish was carried in sheeted open wagons and a 4mm kit is available of this special type of wagon. Locomotives used were allocated to the NB shed at Berwick and were invariably small Drummond 0-6-0T locomotives. After the Grouping, Berwick shed closed and the workings were taken over by Tweedmouth shed: an old NER shed, and larger J21 0-6-0 tender locomotives commenced on the branch.

I have a theory that the J21s' wheel-base was too long for the extremely tight crossover and sometime in the

1920s, it was removed and both passenger and freight workings were then gravity shunted. Apparently, there were very few accidents over the years whilst this practice continued, right up in fact, to closure in 1962. The locomotive would approach the station throat and stop. Brakes would be pinned down on the train whilst the locomotive ran forward into one of the sidings. The coach or wagons would then be allowed to run into another road under gravity, with the guard braking carefully. The locomotive would then run out and commence shunting. In latter days, the locomotive always left Burnmouth tender first and then back up from Eyemouth chimney first.

Typically the track was relayed, including the first two turnouts in 1960 and it is probable that the station building, a delightful standard NB structure, was painted at the same time: consequently the branch closed completely in February 1962!

The only other structures within the station limits were a water tower situated at the platform end and some storage buildings in the yard. The two sidings nearest to the river - Eye Water, were used mainly to store fish vans and a second coach, usually an eight compartment non-corridor, was

stored in here too. It would be pressed into service, possibly at weekends, for the odd through service to Berwick upon Tweed. Atop the buffer stops was an oil store.

A short distance up the line was Biglawburn siding: this was a single siding where originally, local farmers would deliver their produce and collect machinery and supplies. In later days, and certainly up to closure, an oil storage tank was located here and tank wagons were off loaded.

If I was ever to build a layout based upon Eyemouth, it would be set just before closure in 1962 when there was still a fair amount of fish traffic. The passenger coach on the branch since 1952 was a non-corridor Thompson brake composite and Tweedmouth shed's J39s held sway. Some of them had non-standard NER tenders, therefore allowing a little bit of variation.

For those who prefer small branch lines (and they don't come much smaller than Eyemouth) this could make an ideal project. I'll leave it up to you as to how you sort out the gravity shunting, though with the recent advent of DCC control, by putting powered bogies in some wagons, and the passenger brake coach, it might actually be easier now than we ever thought possible!

Eyemouth at a glance

Design scale: 4mm. **Period:** Suitable for pre-grouping up until 1962, depending on personal choice. Note the inclusion of the release crossover in early periods.
Location: East Coast near the Scottish Border. **Locomotive types:** see text.
Typical traffic: Short branch passenger trains, fish, coal, fuel oil and no doubt some general merchandise.

Chapter 4
Ayrshire and the South West

This particular region was in many respects, very similar to the landscape over in the east around Lothian and parts of the Borders. It shared the similar characteristic of a long coastline, but in this case there were more opportunities to develop ports for trade with north west England and Ireland. There was an abundance of mineral wealth in the region, certainly in the northern area close to Glasgow and into Lanarkshire, where there were vast reserves of it. Once again coal became the key reason for the development of the railways and, once mined it could be readily exported through the emerging ports in the area, such as Ardrossan.

Inland, much of the region was turned over to farming and thus sought improved rural and agricultural transport links, though equally, there were tracts of moorland and numerous river valleys which were challenging for the early railway promoters. A number of towns,

already involved in manufacturing, were dotted around the region notably Paisley, Kilmarnock and in the south, Dumfries.

The South West was indeed a vast triangle of land ripe for new transport links. The canals arrived first, with a venture linking Glasgow, Paisley and Ardrossan, although in the end it had only reached Johnstone by 1813. Its promoters realised a better means of transport lay in the new railway system and a line from Johnstone to Ardrossan was proposed in 1827.

Other lines proposed during the 1830s included routes to Kilmarnock, Greenock and Ayr, and soon it was evident that the Ayrshire coast was becoming a magnet to the working people of Glasgow. Railway companies proceeded to build lines up and down the coastline to Largs, Troon, Prestwick and further south at Girvan to exploit the tourist potential. At the same time the mineral deposits mentioned above were opened up with numerous lines crossing

the county of Ayrshire in all directions. Lines also served huge ironworks at Glengarnock and armaments manufacturing close to Irvine.

A major stage in the development of this region was the proposal by the Glasgow, Paisley, Kilmarnock and Ardrossan Railway to build a line linking the capital with Dumfries and Carlisle. It joined forces with the Glasgow, Carlisle and Dumfries Railway in order to consolidate their domain. The company had more or less secured its territory along the coast, or so it had thought, and after a bitter battle with the Caledonian Railway, it secured permission to construct a line

Below: G&SWR layouts are rare, but this exceptional ScaleSeven example built by Ian Middleditch, chairman of the G&SWR Association, helps to redress the balance. 'Auchlin' is a just supposing station on the Ayr and Cumnock route and includes some exchange sidings for the adjacent pit.
(Photograph: Steve Flint)

southwards through the Nith Valley. The Caledonian Railway, in the meantime, was to build its line over Beattock and at Gretna, just north of the border, both companies were to share tracks into Carlisle itself. By now, it was the 1850s, and the company that would operate much of the track mileage in the south west did indeed become known as the Glasgow & South Western Railway.

The Caledonian Railway seemed intent on becoming the most dominant company within Scotland and a continuous state of aggravation existed between the two companies. A look at a pre-grouping railway map will see the Caledonian and G&SWR had a number of lines serving similar locations in the north: an unceasing duplication of railway tracks that must have been expensive to each company.

The various developing railways encouraged tourist traffic to the seaside resorts on the Ayrshire coast, and this continued well into LMS days. Visitors were much reduced after the Second World War, but even today, many of the original resorts are still served by rail, much of it electrified with services running from Glasgow Central.

Often such stations such as Wemyss Bay (CR) and Largs (G&SWR) were provided with ornate glass roofs and canopies typical of late Victorian and Edwardian architecture. Wemyss Bay station was developed along with the pier for Rothesay and the Isle of Bute ferry service. It is quite magnificent to this day and would make a lovely modelling project, suitable for any period, since most of the original station buildings from 1903 (when the Caledonian Railway extended and rebuilt the station), together with the platform canopies and the covered walkway to the adjacent pier are still intact and available for research.

Such stations, whether terminus or through stations, can inspire attractive modelling propositions, either as an historical scale project of a specific place, or combined with other features to develop a 'just supposing' scenario. For instance, a passenger station could be combined with a steamer/ferry pier and a town-sized goods yard in the traditional idiom; a freight only line might also strike off under a bridge and through the backscene to deliver coal for export to a supposed nearby harbour located conveniently offstage, but providing addition operating potential (see plan below). Equally attractive for any period, from pre-grouping to present day.

By the 1980s EMUs would be the norm of course, and the town goods yard would have closed: dormant until a 1990s supermarket development arrived, or a 2000s swish apartment building boom. Through freight to the harbour facility could well have survived though, in the guise of imported iron ore (like Hunterston) or coal for export, or even, in modern times, coal imports. Suitable for 2mm and 4mm, and even 7mm for the adventurous, with the opportunity to include a seaside townscape in the Ayrshire vernacular.

A scheme for the Ayrshire Coast

As described in the main text, the Ayrshire coast provides plenty of just-supposing potential for anyone looking to include a largish maritime feature on a layout. This plan is inspired by Wemyss Bay, Inverclyde, a busy interchange for the island communities of the Firth of Clyde and beyond.

The hidden siding beneath the hill would need to be remotely operated by some means if built against a wall. Tracks could also be extended onto the pier if desired.

Right: the magnificent station buildings at Wemyss Bay seen in the 1950s.
(Photograph: Santona Publications Library)

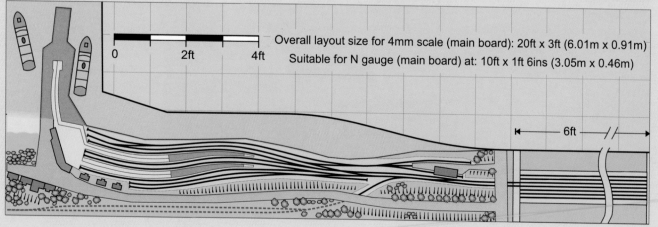

Overall layout size for 4mm scale (main board): 20ft x 3ft (6.01m x 0.91m)
Suitable for N gauge (main board) at: 10ft x 1ft 6ins (3.05m x 0.46m)

0   2ft   4ft

6ft

Returning to the early years, it was then possible to sail across to Ireland and down the coast to England by steamer services. Leaving Glasgow a steamer would sail down the River Clyde to Ardrossan, then continue to Liverpool where passengers could connect with a train to London. Prices between rival shipping companies were slashed in an attempt to gain customers, much like the 'no-frills' airlines of today, really. However, it was to no avail, because Scottish travellers still seemed to prefer the more established Leith to London steamer service. The obvious answer to capturing the patronage was to link, with some urgency, the railways on either side of the border and establish through routes to London and elsewhere.

Right: epitomising the 'Port Road' - an attractive route that is rarely modelled - is this long freight behind a BR Standard Class 4 at Loch Ken in 1964.
(Photograph: Roy M. Crombie)

Below: Newton Stewart was the junction for the Whithorn branch and is seen here in BR days. It would make a sizeable layout project with lots of modelling potential.
(Photograph: Ian Middleditch collection)

The early promoters also saw trade with Ireland being very important. The shortest sea route was across the Irish Sea from Portpatrick, on the southernmost tip of the region. It has been mentioned frequently that the terrain in Scotland was extremely challenging to the early engineers, and one automatically thinks about the routes through the Highlands, or through the Border Country, but rarely is it mentioned that the land between Dumfries, Kirkcudbright and Newton Stewart was equally testing. There were numerous rivers to cross as well as long ascents and descents over high moorland. Nevertheless, a route was proposed to link Dumfries (and therefore Carlisle) with Stranraer and Portpatrick. It was completed in stages, first arriving in

Castle Douglas and then onto Stranraer via New Galloway and Newton Stewart before eventually arriving at Portpatrick in 1862.

The financial difficulties encountered by the local concerns building the latter stretches of the line, and its associated branches, were so great that they were brought together and assisted by the Caledonian, Midland, London and North Western and Glasgow & South Western Railways, the culmination of which was the formation of The Portpatrick and Wigtownshire Joint Railway Company. The involvement of the Midland and LNWR was obvious, as they held sway with railways south of the border and therefore, this had traffic implications for them regarding both passengers and

Left: after closure of the Port Road, heavy freight traffic to Stranraer continued via Kilmarnock. Here, in July 1990, 37 517 heads north near Dailly with an empty steel working from the Stockton Haulage depot in Stranraer.
(Photograph: G. C. O'Hara)

freight to and from Ireland. A little later in 1870, a line reached Portpatrick from Girvan in the north, which itself had been reached via Ayr and Maybole. Traffic for Ireland was now able to arrive from two directions, although due to early disputes, it was the mid 1880s before it grew.

There were two branches off the 'Port Road' as the route became known, and they traversed some beautiful countryside, both eventually ending up on the Solway Coast. The first was from Castle Douglas to Kirkcudbright. The terminus there is quite remarkable, as it would make an excellent model, and as yet I have to see a layout built by someone. It closed to both passenger and freight traffic in 1965. The other branch, slightly longer, was between Newton Stewart and Whithorn, with the addition of a tiny 'twig' of a branch between Millisle and Garlieston. This branch lost its passenger service in 1950, but freight lingered on until 1964. They were distinctly rural lines carrying livestock, agricultural merchandise, coal and milk from local creameries. Towards the end, they became the preserve of the BR Standard Class 2MT locomotives, although prior to this the Caledonian Railway standard 0-6-0 goods locomotives had also been seen on the Monday, Wednesday and Friday trip workings. Numerous photographs of this delightful little terminus

have been published and, as I alluded to above, I still wonder why no-one has ever tackled this as a layout project.

Eventually Stranraer became the main port in the locality, because of the shelter offered to shipping by Loch Ryan, and the Portpatrick extension closed in 1950. However, because of the importance of the Port Road route, many express trains and boat trains were operated by quite large locomotives, including Black Fives and BR Standard Class 4 engines. LMS Crabs and Clan Pacifics were common visitors whilst an assortment of smaller locomotives, including pre-grouping types, performed on freight services. Closure of the main line came in 1965, and whilst diesels never really got a foothold on services, it was Type 2 diesel classes that hauled the demolition trains. Dumfries Motive Power Depot lost many of its duties when the Port Road closed and consequently it too closed in 1966. A short spur to the oil sidings at Maxwelltown still remains in-situ I believe, as it was part of the original Speedlink scheme.

By any stretch of the imagination, the Port Road has escaped the attention of modellers for years. Notwithstanding Whithorn and Kirkcudbright, the Solway coast provides all sort of might-have-been destinations for branch lines in the steam age; Port William, Port Logan and Carsluith to name but a few, and all in an attractive scenic coastal setting. Just supposing too, that the strategic importance of the route was realised before Beeching got his way and it survived to this day. If it had done, it would have been principally a through freight route, perhaps with a modest social needs passenger service

Left: the terminus at Kirkcudbright in 1963 sees a BR Standard 4MT, No. 80023, with a pair of Stanier 'Porthole' coaches forming a train for Dumfries. Surrounded by traditional Scottish town houses and the Parish Church (just out of shot on the left), the station offers great potential for a historical branch terminus project.
(Photograph: Derek Cross, cty. David M. Cross)

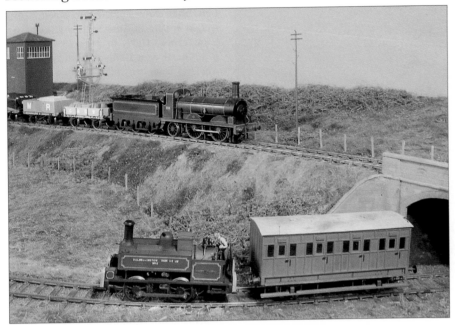

and surely a sleeper service up until the late 1980s. Plenty of food for thought, with the occasional castle on the back-drop and attractive vernacular cottages along the lineside, who could resist?

Meanwhile back in the heart of the region in pre-grouping times, the Caledonian Railway penetrated through to Ardrossan, sending most of its coal traffic via their line from Rutherglen. The Caledonian aimed to provide its own central route through Barrhill and Kilwinning and this was opened in 1888. Naturally the G&SWR were unhappy about such penetration into their territory by the CR, and they proceeded to utilise running rights into collieries in NBR territory around Lanarkshire. However, so much competition only resulted in the colliery owners benefiting from some extremely low tariffs!

As I have said above, from a modelling point of view, the region as a whole seems to be quite a neglected area. For quite sometime now, it seems a lone furrow has been ploughed by Ian and Kenneth Middleditch up in Ayrshire, with their ScaleSeven G&SWR layouts, of which their Auchlin branch is featured here. When one considers the variety of terrain and possible operating scenarios, I am surprised at the lack of layouts. Perhaps the G&SWR has not attracted the attention the other Scottish line groups have, although I feel sure members of the G&SWR Association

would tend to disagree with that remark! There was much mineral traffic to consider, including vast numbers of private owner wagons, whilst even today the coal traffic is still flourishing, with imports and exports being carried from the new open cast sites and loading facilities in the north of the region.

Examination of a map of G&SWR routes reveals that there were not many archetypal branch line terminii: most 'branches' were secondary through routes, so perhaps that's one reason why modellers have kept away. Dalmellington is the celebrated example of course, with numerous photographs, often depicting the Park Royal railbus in service in the latter days of the branch. There are numerous through stations of branch line size however, though photographs do seem to be hard to come by. The G&SWR Association has produced a station register which includes some diagrams, nevertheless, there are tracts within the south west that are untouched by the iron road and a glimpse across a map of the area will reveal settlements that just might-have-been served by a railway had history been a little different; Glentrool, Dalquhairn and Carsphairn for example. The Caledonian could have struck out across the terrain as well: they reached Ardrossan, so why not Ayr?

To redress the balance a bit I am including a couple of photograph panels illustrating examples of G&SWR branch lines (right) and a miscellany of G&SWR structures (overleaf).

Today many of the seaside routes are still operating with short EMU trains although the stations served, including some of the terminus stations, are a little bare of structures and frequently have all

Above: railways were constructed in this sparsely populated region to exploit the coal reserves, thus an industrial connection off a remote moorland branch line is perfectly feasible, as portrayed on Auchlin. The afternoon 'Paddy' train to the offstage pit is seen headed by an 0-4-0PT built by Hawthorn of Leith in 1851.

Left: Auchlin station building is based on the wooden sectional design that seems to be unique to the Glasgow & South Western Railway (see 'Rankinston' opposite, and 'Fairlie' on page 21)
(Photographs: Steve Flint)

G&SWR Branch Lines

I mentioned in the main text that this region had few traditional branch line terminii, and that could be a reason why the patch appears to be so neglected by layout builders. Hopefully the few shots assembled here, along with the 'Auchlin' shots, will go some way to show that very modellable prototypes did exist in this part of Scotland. The stations would, for those who want to model a 'real place', make attractive layouts in their own right, whereas selecting their essential features to create a composition of one's own would work equally well.

Top: the station at Patna, on the Dalmellington branch shows the original platform in the foreground with its replacement beyond. Note the goods shed and siding are accessible directly from the running lines.

Centre: this LMS period shot of Rankinston shows the G&SWR sctional timber building design to good effect.
(Photographs: Ian Middleditch collection)

Below: Drongan station c. 1970, seen before closure to freight. The tubular post signals were probably installed when the branch to Killoch Colliery was opened in 1960. *(Photograph: Stuart Rankin)*

Right: in contrast to the timber station building design (see pages 21 and 45), more substantial stone-built structures were provided on the G&SWR's main routes such as at New Cumnock, photographed c.1972, when it had clearly seen better days. *(Photographs: Stuart Rankin)*

Centre right: island platform structures are always attractive and the one at Kilbarchan (centre right) photographed in more halcyon times is a fine example. The route is now closed and the structure long since demolished.

(Photograph: Ian Middleditch collection)

Below: The signal box at Holywood is clearly G&SWR style though with a brick lower storey.

Lower left: many G&SWR goods sheds were timber built as this example at Auchlinleck illustrates.

Lower right: modelling detail, a standard panelled overbridge at Drongan.

(Photographs: Stuart Rankin)

Kilbarchan Station.

Above: Ayr station sees a visit by an LMS 2P 4-4-0, No. 616, in the grouping years. The 2Ps were especially prevalent on the G&SWR from 1926 until the late 1950s.
(Photograph: Santona Publications Library)

Below: as is evident throughout this book, modelling the pre-grouping scene in Scotland usually requires some kit or scratchbuilding of locomotives and stock. The results speak for themselves however, as Auchlin, which recreates magnificently the G&SWR in Edwardian Scotland, so ably demonstrates here.
(Photograph: Steve Flint)

Haulage which brought other heavy diesel motive power to the area.

More recently, Strathclyde PTE orange and black liveried Sprinter Class 156 units could be seen, some operating on quite long distance service diagrams. For instance, I remember operating my 'Newcastle Haymarket' P4 layout with one such unit. A visitor at a show intimated that it was not prototypical to do so until I was able to produce a photograph showing such units at Newcastle Central station and along the Tyne Valley on through services to Stranraer! At one point I do believe the service was actually named.

First Scotrail still serve the region, and Stranraer Harbour station has been intriguingly modernised with a new roof and glass canopies, but a dip into the histories of the Glasgow & South Western and Caledonian Railways will reveal that taking a greater interest in this part of world could result in an absorbing project: certainly one that would be different from the usual Scottish genre layouts observed in the model press or at exhibitions, for which I am perhaps guilty of perpetrating myself!

Intensive operation out of Glasgow to seaside resorts, Pacific locomotives on the Port Road, mineral traffic a plenty including the present day, what more do you need?

the atmosphere of a bus stop! But that should not deter those of more modern persuasion: in the 1960s and 1970s the distinctive Class 126 DMUs were characteristic of the Ayr and Stranraer areas and when they were withdrawn there was a short interlude of loco haulage on the Stranraer boat trains which brought Class 27s more extensively than before. Later on, 47s took over, with distinctive Sealink-liveried Mk1 coaches for a short period. As mentioned in the photograph caption on page 43, a steel terminal was operated at Stranraer by Stockton

Chapter 5

The Central Belt

Towards the end of the 18th century, Edinburgh and Glasgow were becoming the commercial capitals of the country. They were but forty-five miles apart in what was later to become known as the Central Belt of Scotland. Edinburgh lay by the banks of the Firth of Forth whilst over in the west, Glasgow lay astride the River Clyde, and emerged as the country's industrial hub, becoming a manufacturing centre and seaport. In Edinburgh, the main port was nearby at Leith and the trade was mainly with countries on the other side of the North Sea, known as the German Sea in those days. However, at that time, it was possible to sail up the Firth of Forth as far as Stirling, so there were plenty of opportunities for goods to be sent by sea to destinations all around the globe.

As we have discovered, the first railways or wagon-ways were used to transport coal and minerals down to these great tracts of water. For example: coal was being sent from the Dunfermline area by wagon-way to Rosyth on the north bank of the Forth as early as the 1760s. Iron was being produced from blast furnaces near Falkirk at much the same period. Canals were the first main method of carrying minerals and finished goods within the Central Belt. However,

they were not always the most direct way to send goods, so it was natural that an extension of the wooden railed wagon-ways would eventually take place. Cast-iron rails were by now being utilised by the collieries.

To the east of Glasgow, an area known as the Monklands Plateau was rich in minerals and by the early 19th century it was being exploited by colliery owners and ironmasters. It was to the south of the great Forth and Clyde canal, and soon wagon-ways were winding their way down to that canal via the route of the Monklands Canal. However in 1824, an Act of Parliament was passed allowing a railway called the Monkland and Kirkintilloch Railway to be built. The aim of this railway, the first in Scotland authorised to utilise steam power, was to encompass, and feed the produce of, the Monklands area into the canal system. In 1831, the Garnick and Glasgow railway linked into the Monkland and Kirkintilloch Railway, and it put itself in direct competition with the canal systems, providing a much quicker and direct route to transport coal and minerals into Glasgow itself. Scotland's railways were thus born from these early concerns which not only transported goods and minerals, but passengers too.

Thoughts to link the main centres of population commenced with lines being planned in 1837 between Glasgow, Paisley, Kilmarnock, Ayr and Greenock. The first mainline between the two great cities, Edinburgh and Glasgow, was authorised in 1838 and all of these routes were open for business by 1842. There were plans to unite with railways being constructed in England and many routes around the coasts and through the borders were being investigated. By 1845, 'Railway Mania' was in full swing with daily announcements in the press regarding new schemes. Many were doomed to fail: they were frequently rural affairs and the early promoters had little or no knowledge on how to build and operate a railway. Whilst it is nowadays easy to see the urban sprawl of Scotland's towns and cities, it must be remembered that during the mid-nineteenth century, if you say, walked one or two miles from the centres of population, you would be in the middle of the countryside.

Below: My 'Lochside' layout of the late 1970s was set on north Clydeside and although I mainly operated it with blue diesels, the clock was occasionally set back to the 1950s, as seen here with an ex-NBR Glen 4-4-0 (a GEM kit) in use.
(Photograph: the author)

Thus, a year or so later, and the number of new schemes had dwindled and settled down to a more balanced state of development. By the 1850s, three Anglo-Scottish routes across the Border were commencing operation and soon the gradual amalgamation of smaller concerns was starting to take place. Within the Central Belt and indeed beyond, three major companies were becoming responsible for the railways. The North British Railway, its great rival the Caledonian Railway and the smaller, but equally important Glasgow and South Western Railway, were taking control. Occasionally these companies clashed as they competed for territory but in many respects that only assisted the way the railways grew in Scotland and shaped the eventual network.

It would take a complete book in itself to explore the various lines which grew up in and around the Central Belt. But grow they did, and the railway companies actually played quite an important part in the prosperity of the region. Nearly all of the companies realised that the huge number of people needed to keep industry moving, especially in Glasgow and Edinburgh, all required housing. Within the actual industrial areas, that was becoming more difficult to achieve. The middle management and 'white collar' workers did not want to be living in the slum areas around the factories and shipyards. As a result the railway companies built lines to more rural locations but still within easy reach of the workplaces. Lots of new houses, especially villas, started to appear further west, along both sides

of the River Clyde, and in the Paisley and Kilbride area to name but two localities. Whole estates and settlements grew up and of course the railways were able to transport the people. Thus, the suburban or commuter railway was born in Scotland: and to this day is still the principal reason for the existence of much of the railway system in this region.

Contemporary with all the railway growth was a network of ferries operating on the River Clyde to take businessmen into the city. The railway companies saw this as competition and started to operate their own vessels along the river. Within the great centres of population they also had to deal with competition from tramways. The very nature of the tramway enabled passengers an easier, more convenient and

Central Belt suburban routes.

With generally shorter train lengths the Glasgow and Edinburgh suburban lines are worth considering for modelling. The island platforms of the Cathcart Circle stations have a particular appeal, as with Mount Florida (right) seen in 1955, whilst the twin platforms of the Edinburgh suburban line, here at Morningside Road in 1962, are almost mirror images. Goods traffic could be created on an independent lower-level section of layout, as was often the case with these routes around Glasgow. *(Photographs: W. A. C. Smith)*

usually cheaper means to reach their workplace; both Glasgow and Edinburgh had extensive tram routes and some of the early railways succumbed to the competition and closed. Nevertheless, many of the suburban services operated frequent fast services into the city and several terminus stations were built as a result. There has however been a gradual consolidation of lines over the years and many of the fine pre-grouping terminal stations have gone. Certainly there was quite a number of terminii built in both Edinburgh and Glasgow and many of them are not well known. The main stations in Glasgow included the North British Railway terminus, Queen Street, whilst the nearby terminus of Buchanan Street was operated by the Caledonian Railway. From the south trains crossed the River Clyde to enter the Caledonian Central Station, whilst a further station

was eventually built at St Enoch, which served the Glasgow and South Western lines. That is the most simplistic means of showing the ownership of the terminus stations in Glasgow. In reality, many of Glasgow's railways consisted of amalgamations with joint lines and running rights. Only Queen Street and Central remain today, the other two stations closing in the 1960s (see panel, page 53).

In Edinburgh it was simpler since only the Caley and the NBR served the city. Waverley Station was the main focus and was originally operated by the North British. The Caledonian had less influence in the city, and had its terminus at Princes Street which closed in 1964. However, within Leith, both the NBR and CR had extensive networks, and several passenger terminii. One particularly delightful NBR station was at North Leith. It was extremely compact and has

been modelled on a number of occasions, including a recent offering from Bob and Gareth Rowlands (below).

The Caledonian had a branch to Barnton whilst the North British had a whole series of rural branch lines radiating from Waverley. They also had a circular route around the city, and every now and again plans are raised to re-open those lines again. Edinburgh Waverley also received main line services from the north and from across the border.

Across the Central Belt a number of lines linked the two cities either directly or indirectly. The network has diminished considerably over the years with the ex-North British lines suffering possibly the most. Only the truncated Bathgate branch remains, along with the main route through Falkirk High, Polmont and Linlithgow, and a loop through Falkirk Grahamston. Of the closed lines many

The lines through Leith and Granton were truly urban ones, squeezed into compact sites and often running in walled cuttings surrounded by tall tenement buildings and warehouses. 'Scotland Street' by Dave Elbourne and 'North Leith' (below) by Bob and Gareth Rowlands are both authentic adaptations of the respective prototypes.

Left: North Leith in 1927 sees a suburban service for Edinburgh headed by an ex-NBR Holmes 4-4-0T No 10467.
(Photograph: R. W. Lynn Collection)

Right: Carstairs Junction in 2006 is either the epitome of the modern railway, or a shadow of its former self, depending on your viewpoint! If you do not like structure modelling, then a modern day layout based on this locality would suit those interested in stock and operation.
(Photograph: Steve Flint)

were principally for freight, in particular, the Caledonian branches to the south east of Glasgow serving the collieries as far down as the Douglas Coalfield, although a few lines remain open for open-cast mining today. The main line through Motherwell, Law Junction and onto Carstairs Junction provides an electrified route between Edinburgh and Glasgow, indeed the Nottingham Bulwell Society built a 1980s/90s period layout based on the junction sections.

For devotees of steam operation, many of the lines servicing the collieries of the ex-NB and CR network in this region would make interesting layouts. Of course, the intensive workings would require large numbers of mineral wagons and depending upon the period selected, many of the colourful private owner wagons could be used. Some pretty vintage motive power could also be incorporated, although a few pits did remain open long enough to be served by diesel locomotives. In particular, the 1990s saw vast amounts of coal and coal by-products being shipped to the 1960s-built power stations at Cockenzie and Longannet. Some new sections of track were built during this period and the resurgent traffic saw the introduction of Class 56s and 60s into Scotland. Methil power station in Fife had particularly interesting workings. It had been designed to burn low-grade

fuel, initially coal slurry supplied in block trains of 21T or 24½T mineral wagons, then in the 1980s, waste coal from bings was used, conveyed in redundant MSV aggregate tipplers. By the mid-1990s these had been replaced by mixed rakes of SSA and MEA box wagons. These lighter duties still provided work for Class 26 and 37 locomotives.

Of course, other bulk freight - oil and its derivatives - has been sent all over Scotland from the refineries at Grangemouth for decades. This offers lots of alternative periods to tempt modellers with a particular interest in this traffic. For instance, during the British Rail era the ex–Caledonian Railway locomotive shed at Grangemouth was host to a variety of typical Scottish diesel motive power, including the Sulzer-engined Type 2s as well as Class 20s and 37s. Even today the fuel oil traffic is busy out of Grangemouth Refinery.

Sticking with the British Rail era for a moment, as I believe this period is (at the time of writing) is in its ascendancy as a modelling favourite: it is not only the block trains of coal and oil which have to be considered. The introduction of Speedlink services in the late 1970s resurrected wagonload traffic in contemporary air-braked vehicles and rail freight was often sent to outlying parts of the network in batches consisting of only one or two wagons. For the modeller this makes the 1980s and early 1990s an interesting period for freight operations

Examples of Central Belt rail freight activity. Below left: a Hapag Lloyd container train at Greenock. 37025 is in action with the Firth of Clyde forming a splendid backdrop.

Below: van traffic is always a firm favourite for a layout, especially this! 26031 shunts the siding at the Hill Street plant of Johnny Walker, Kilmarnock, in 1987.
(Photographs: George C. O'Hara)

throughout the whole of the Central Belt. The hub for Speedlink operations in Scotland was the marshalling yard at Mossend between Coatbridge and Motherwell. The list of products sent by rail during that period is very comprehensive and included; fuel oil, china clay, coal, coal products, caustic soda, finished paper products, aluminium ingots, alumina, grain, bricks, foodstuffs including canned drinks, molasses, steel (both coiled and flat), iron ore, timber, government stores, fertilizer, carbon dioxide, ammonia, limestone, pet food and of course, Scotland's most famous export – whisky!

A lot of the above commodities (such as china clay, caustic soda and ammonia etc.) were moved in purpose built wagons, many of which are, unfortunately, not available as ready to run models, but a fair proportion was transported in the British Rail standard air braked types; the OAA and OBA 20ft 9in wheelbase opens, and their cousins the VAA/VBA and VDA covered vans. These were introduced during the 1970s along with the larger continental style bogie Cargowaggons. The OCA opens and VGA vans followed in the 1980s and became the cornerstone of Speedlink services throughout the 1980s.

I can certainly remember observing such traffic during my visits up to Scotland in the 1980s, before departing to a new job in the Midlands, and of course, many such trains during this period were trip workings consisting of just a few wagons - an ideal scenario if you want to work in 7mm scale, but have limited space.

Other than the yard at Perth, the largest marshalling facilities were concentrated within the Central Belt. Perth, together with Millerhill near Edinburgh, was developed as part of the national railway freight strategy in the 1955 Modernisation Plan. Perth soon became a 'white elephant', but Millerhill remained busy until the abandonment of the Speedlink network. A yard at Cadder, north-east of Glasgow, was a staging point for the West Highland Line in particular, but the real hub for Speedlink operations in Scotland was the yard at Mossend. It had been constructed by the LMS, but came to prominence in respect of traffic associated with steelmaking, when the nearby Ravenscraig works opened in 1956.

Today (2006) Ravenscraig is long closed but much of the current freight is still dealt with at Mossend, utilising the electrified West Coast Main Line as the major freight route between England and Scotland.

The present trend for rail-road freight exchange facilities within Scotland (and even further afield, I'm sure) is to simply concrete a section of land over and lay one or two adjacent sidings. Add a quick-build portal frame warehouse, or maybe just a Portacabin™ office, and some security fencing and you have an instant distribution centre. Not perhaps a scene reflecting the good old days, but one which offers an ideal modelling cameo if your interest encompasses more contemporary practice. Rail managers are constantly attempting to gain or regain new traffic flows and these centres are springing up all over the place. The simplest of them only require a suitable mobile crane to remove containers from the wagons (see my Georgemas scheme on page 76) Fortunately the 4mm model railway manufacturers have latched onto this and some suitable rolling stock is becoming available. The theme also creates an opportunity to utilise the many realistic model lorries now found on the market.

Whilst focusing on freight and speaking of the good old days, that is: the steam era, as some would have it! The bulk of the goods trains then seen in most parts of Scotland consisted of varieties of open or mineral wagons and box vans. Naturally there were numerous specialist wagons, dependent on precise location, but the period of the pick-up goods, which still existed at most British Railway stations until the Beeching rationalisation of the 1960s, still relied upon traditional short-wheelbase vehicles. Fortunately, there are plenty of such vehicles available for modellers, especially in the more popular scales. And whilst the major manufacturers are developing their ranges, other types are still only available in kit form, some in injection-moulded plastic and others in etched brass or nickel silver.

As mentioned previously, the Central Belt region is where the main line terminus stations are situated. One of my favourite locations, where I simply stand and watch the trains moving about, is Glasgow Central station. There seems to be a traffic movement every minute or so with suburban DMUs and EMUs, as well as the long distance trains gliding over the maze of trackwork. It is of course a huge station and would require considerable space even in N Gauge. Some of the other big terminus stations in Glasgow could be adapted though, and I have briefly examined some options in the panel, right.

Steelworks Traffic

Steel production in Scotland became concentrated at the BSC Ravenscraig site near Motherwell. It was a huge complex incorporating many smaller works and its traffics would obviously be suited to the larger layout. Inwards came limestone from Hardendale near Shap, later supplemented by dolofines from Thrislington, Durham. In the 1980s, both flows used 100 ton PTA bogie tipplers, although the Shap traffic also used large four-wheelers christened 'white ladies'. Iron ore was imported initially through General Terminus Quay (seen right, in 1978) in dedicated $33^1/_2$T hoppers. From 1980, the traffic transferred to Hunterston deep water terminal and utilised block trains of PTA rotary tippler wagons. *(Photograph: George C. O'Hara)*

Modelling a city terminus

For modellers seeking city style main line passenger/parcels operations, there are several terminus stations in the Glasgow area that can be adapted. For instance, the current track formation at Glasgow Queen Street only requires seven turnouts to recreate its station throat. It could be adapted so as to show a station in a tight site surrounded by high retaining walls, perhaps like a northern version of C. J. Freezer's classic 'Minories' plan. Ex-NB, Queen Street has always had an intensive service, including in recent times, the push-pull operations between the Nation's capitals. West Highland services have long originated here too, and of course, the notorious climb out of the station up Cowlairs bank meant that many outbound trains required banking assistance - now achieved easily and realistically with DCC. Overall, an adaptation of Queen Street would offer an intensive operating scheme with plenty of loco haulage in steam or diesel days, and all in a comparatively narrow space.

More grandiose, but one that could be developed with selective compression is the former G&SWR terminus, St Enoch, seen below in a careworn state shortly before closure.

With its huge curved overall roofs, it lends itself well as a prototype on which to base a major pre-grouping project in 4mm, perhaps in the style of Peter Denny's Buckingham (which was essentially a compact version of the GCR Marylebone terminus). A lot of kit or scratchbuilding of stock would be be necessary, so it would be a long term project requiring a lot of motivation to see through to the finish.

Finally, why not consider Buchanan Street (not illustrated), with easy to build canopies rather than an overall roof. Like St Enoch, it closed in the mid-1960s, but it would be appropriate for utilising the current 4mm transition era locomotives and stock on offer from the big manufacturers (for instance A4s, V2s, BR Standard Class 5s and ex-LMS Black 5s, intermixed with diesels including class 40s, 21s and other Type 2s).

Left: the heavy traffic crammed onto the overbridge above Glasgow Queen Street gives this photograph an almost layout-like appearance. 47707 is seen at the head of a Glasgow-Edinburgh push -pull train in February 1980.
(Photograph: Steve Flint)

Centre: 27201 bursts into the sunshine with an ex-Edinburgh service in August 1975. The tunnels and retaining walls would provide an easily constructed backdrop and scenic break for the layout.
(Photograph: Ian Fleming)

Below: Glasgow St Enoch at the end of its days. This ex-G&SWR terminus must have been a magnificent sight in its days of glory. It would be a major undertaking to reproduce it in any scale: any takers?
(Photograph Stuart Rankin)

However, as we shall see over the next few pages, in direct contrast to main line terminii, a compact urban terminus can provide interesting operation too, and by utilising the correct rolling stock, it can be easily identified as to its general location. By looking at current or past rail network maps, you can also choose the destinations where you want your trains to run to and much of the rail network, especially on the surviving suburban routes, has now been electrified. Fortunately, the 4mm scale market has recently seen (at the time of writing in 2006) developments by DC Kits and Bratchell Models, including the introduction of suitable Scottish Region EMUs and DMUs. They are not particularly cheap and do require assembly and related skills, but now provide prospective Scottish urban modellers with correct pattern rolling stock for their layouts.

There are also quite a number of junction stations or simply junctions themselves, which could provide you with suitable inspiration for a model. The triangular junction just south of Larbert, close to Falkirk is an interesting affair, set as it is, in a semi-rural location and still operated with semaphore signals. Even

Helensburgh Central Survey

My particular interest in matters West Highland took me to Helensburgh one day in order to photograph Helensburgh Upper on the line itself. It took only a matter of minutes to carry out this task, so I headed back into the town, parked the car and went in search of sustenance, in particular, a 'Bridie', of which I am particularly fond! I decided to wander about a bit, munching the bridie and looking out for postcards. I invariably send these postcards to the far-flung corners of the world, strange I know! Anyhow, I turned a corner, and to my surprise I stumbled across Helensburgh Central station, slap bang in the middle of the town. For some unforgivable reason, I had totally forgotten such a station existed. It was stupid of me, because when you have an 'upper' station, surely there must be another station in the locality.

Naturally, the 'Central' station required investigation, and I immediately saw a future layout in its design. It had been quite a large station in steam days, with its own depot next to the station. Electrification of the North Clyde lines

in 1960 ensured the steam depot was swept away, but Helensburgh Central has remained much as it was, as a compact, self-contained suburban terminus station. It is now in its most basic form, three platform faces served by two slightly curved turnouts, set in a narrow approach surrounded by assorted buildings and greenery with at least two steep foot or road bridges, which make the perfect disguised exit to a set of hidden sidings. At some point after the

Above: the goods yard and locomotive shed at Helensburgh were situated on the north side of the passenger station. This 1950s view shows a wealth of detail for anyone contemplating a period layout. All that can be seen is now lost beneath the park-and-ride car park.
(Photograph: R. W. Lynn collection)

Below: two 2005 views showing the ornate station canopies now thankfully restored to their former glory.
(Photographs: Steve Flint)

within the cities of Glasgow and Edinburgh, such junctions can be found, and their trackwork is often of Setrack™ proportions due to the cramped nature of the site. The junctions close to the new Eastfield Depot could be said to fall into this category too, but there are many including the lines in and around the Leith area of Edinburgh. An SPT Day-Pass will soon allow you to discover a few of these locations and give you prototypical inspiration. Failing that, two books in the Irwell Press series; An Illustrated History of Glasgow's Railways by W. A. C. Smith (ISBN 1 871608 33 3) and, An Illustrated History of Edinburgh's Railways by Paul Anderson (ISBN 1 871608 59 7) contain useful maps, photographs and historical detail, mostly relating to steam operations in the various locations, although many of the lines are still in operation today, of course.

Commuter line operations abound within this region and include a number of seaside and holiday resort destinations, particularly on the banks of the Clyde Estuary. Many routes did close in the '50s and '60s but some still survive. One of my particular favourites is Helensburgh Central, presented here.

electrification was introduced, there were two further storage sidings for EMUs behind the train shed to the north of the site, but they have since been removed.

The station façade and delicate canopies are still there to delight the eye, and no doubt they would make a tremendous soldering task, but it is in remarkable condition, so no broken glass panes or flaky paintwork here. SPT take an enormous pride in their infrastructure and should be praised for their efforts. Signalling is in the shape of three colour light units, easy enough to source in most scales. As it stands even today, Helensburgh Central would make an interesting modern-day project and thus I have no hesitation in presenting this short survey. Even some of the rolling stock is available, certainly as kits in 4mm scale, and would look the part finished in the attractive Strathclyde 'blood and custard' livery. We are talking EMUs of course, and if the layout was backdated to the 1960s, the classic Class 303 'Blue Trains' could be utilised. Backdate to the 1950s, and steam could be utilised in the form of V1 and V3 tank locomotives on suburban coaching stock. In fact that re-occurred in the spring of 1961, when the then new the electric stock was withdrawn for about a year after some of the units caught fire in service.

Above: two shots illustrating the very compact site at the stop-block end.
(Photographs: Steve Flint)

Below left: the entrance to the car park off Princes Street East.

Below: the overbridge over the station throat provides the ideal (if not hackneyed) scenic break for the layout.
(Photographs: the author)

VICTORIA PARK

Victoria Park is to the same track plan as Helensburgh Central or at least very similar, with the same style of buildings and of course those exquisite canopies, but where is it? I have relocated it more or less into the centre of Glasgow on the site of a previously closed North British terminus. A railway to Whiteinch was opened in 1874, but in light of housing development and industrial use, the NBR expanded the station in 1897 calling it Whiteinch Victoria Park. It continued to serve the needs of the area until 1951 although it remained as a storage and goods depot until the late 1960s. As a matter of interest, the actual parkland called 'Victoria Park' is still in existence, hence my name for the layout.

Turn the clock forward and imagine urban regeneration has taken place in the immediate area. Suppose the old station had not been demolished and the old operating authority, Strathclyde PTE, decided that the newly settled population in the new classy flats and apartments needed a transport link into the offices of central Glasgow. Thus the terminus was reopened as just simply 'Victoria Park' to suit the image of the revitalised locality. The line could link into the North Clyde electrified at old Whiteinch Junction with routes into the centre of the city via Partick and Queen St. Lower stations, as well as further routes up through Anniesland, Maryhill and Lochburn (lovely name!), before heading out to perhaps Edinburgh or Stirling, thus offering a cross-city route out to the east and north.

The latter destination, Stirling, could not have been reached by EMUs,

Victoria Park at a glance
Design scale: 7mm, adaptable to 2mm & 4mm. **Location:** Urban Glasgow. **Suggested period:** 1980s, or present day. **Locomotive types:** DMUs (or EMUs), 08, 37 or 66, 67, depending on period. **Typical traffic:** cross-city passenger services, Royal Mail and parcel traffic.

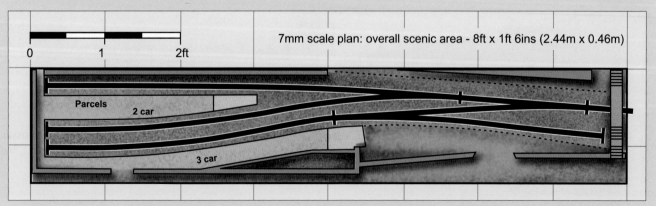

7mm scale plan: overall scenic area - 8ft x 1ft 6ins (2.44m x 0.46m)

0   1   2ft

Parcels

2 car

3 car

Above: Gourock station is less attractive than Helensburgh, but has good services to the rest of the Glasgow Suburban network. The adjacent pier for the Dunoon ferry demonstrates that not all Scottish based layouts with a nautical theme need be in a romanticised Highland setting. An urban scenario, with modern EMUs and some careworn architecture, is equally feasible.
(Photographs: Steve Flint)

so perhaps the station has not been electrified and contemporary DMUs operate the services. That makes it a little simpler for construction too. Now that the Class 150 DMUs have left Scotland, it leaves the three main types; Class 156 in three different liveries (original Scotrail, new 'Barbie' Scotrail and Strathclyde livery) Class 158 in a similar style of paintwork and the newer Class 170 units. Most of these units can be obtained either new or second hand, in both 4mm scale and 2mm scale, although some re-painting may be necessary if you really want to model the latest scene. Likewise, they can be detailed up to a high standard using the various detailing kits on the market (and it should only be a matter of time before Hornby re-release the old Lima 156 DMU). Two or three car sets would be the norm so the station platforms need to be at least a metre or so long to accommodate them. The layout will be quite narrow, possibly only a foot or so wide, making it an ideal project for a bedroom, or along the side of a shed or garage.

I have introduced a short kick-back siding off platform one. This is to store a locomotive or perhaps a permanent way wagon or two and provide a little variety. You could suppose that the Royal Mail was still loading a couple of parcels vans each night, for onward tripping to a larger depot somewhere in Glasgow. Thus a Class 66 or 67 idling in the short siding (with digital

sound perhaps?) would add interest. As an aside, the re-introduction of the Hornby(Lima) Class 101 DMU could possibly be the stimulus to back-date the a layout to the '60s or '70s.

Quite an intensive amount of operation would be possible and a suitably sized set of hidden sidings would be required. However, with the DCC option, storing more than one DMU set on a siding eliminates the multiple isolation switching required with conventional DC control systems and allows more prototypical operating too. Colour light signals and perhaps station platform lighting would give an opportunity to simulate night-time operation, including those nocturnal parcels workings.

My own version of 'Victoria Park' is being built to 7mm scale and I include a couple of views of it still under construction using Peco flat-bottom track. The roadway alongside the station is modelled at the front, whilst at the rear I envisage one of two possible scenes; a modern warehouse feature, similar to those found in many old station yards, or a typical Scottish FA Third Division type of football stand. The latter I would prefer to incorporate although not perhaps on match day: the thought and cost of providing numerous cast figures and painting them all with football scarves and similar attire, does not really bear thinking about!

"Lets be having you Parkies!"

It has fine canopies along the platforms and the main structure is unchanged from steam days. True, it has lost some sidings and the locomotive depot, but its original character is still to be found in what remains. Today's simplistic track layout features in my compact urban terminus plan, Victoria Park (left), although my design depicts a DMU-operated station.

My earlier essays in both 4mm and 7mm regarding the fictitious 'Lochside' saga (see track plan on page 9) were also heavily based upon operations on the north bank of the Clyde and featuring services into central Glasgow along with motive power from Eastfield depot.

Across the River Clyde and you have the stations at Greenock Princess Pier and Gourock adjacent to the pier slipway for the Dunoon ferry. The station (above) is a shadow of its former self, ripe for some architectural upgrading which will surely come in time, but does lend itself to a scheme involving a nautical theme as a scenic adjunct.

However for sheer magnificence, the coastal location at Wemyss Bay, originally constructed by the Greenock and Wemyss Railway in 1865 is simply stunning (see page 41).

Further out, the Largs and Ardrossan trains operate into Glasgow Central, but here we are getting closer to true Glasgow & South Western territory, which I covered in the previous chapter.

Back in the east, most of the lines in

and around Granton and Leith were linked to the freight workings at the docks there. Passenger traffic did exist, although much of it was withdrawn by the 1960s. Further rural branch lines went out to Macmerry, Gullane, North Berwick, Haddington and Gifford: these were mentioned in the Border Country chapter. Close to the zoo in Edinburgh was the short Corstorphine branch, the station for the zoo being the quaintly named Pinkhill. This branch often saw large locomotives such as A4s and V2s on 'filling in' turns. The south side loop also had a frequent suburban service whilst the terminus at St Leonards, nestling beneath Arthur's Seat, was a rather large coal depot with considerable siding space. It was enclosed on one side by some rather forbidding warehouses and was once part of the Edinburgh to Dalkeith Railway, built to a gauge of 4ft 6in and originally operated by horse-power.

For modellers totally interested in locomotives, be it steam, diesel or electric, the Central Belt had the greatest concentration of locomotive depots and stabling points within Scotland. Many of the depots were very large and held vast numbers of locomotives. For those of us interested in steam, the recently introduced Ian Allan re-prints of locomotive allocations in the 1950s are invaluable. Both the Ian Allan and Platform 5 'spotter style' books can help modellers to utilise the correct rolling stock for their layouts. This extends to DMU and EMU allocations too.

However, if big loco sheds are not your bag, there is the potential for supposition of much smaller depots, sheds and stabling points.

Such settings are particularly suited to provide an excellent platform for displaying your collection of locomotives in a small area, and can be tailored to suit

whatever size, shape or power you choose. I have constructed two such layouts in 7mm scale, and one of them, 'Lochty Road' (see page 11 for a brief description) consisted of only three sidings. One of the tracks had a modern style locomotive shed along part of its length, whilst the other two sidings and headshunt had an assortment of isolation sections, in order to hold and store locomotives. Behind the retaining walls, which surrounded the depot, was a small hidden siding sector plate. I assumed the layout was a sub-shed of Eastfield and operated it with typical examples of stock from the early 1980s. It was also gratifying to find many modellers brought to exhibitions their own locomotives, and this allowed us to have many visiting items of rolling stock on display. This layout actually lives on in Scotland together with the 7mm version of 'Lochside' - the two layouts were both

Some Central Belt layouts

Numerous other modellers have been inspired by the the Central Belt over the years. I have already mentioned a few, here are some others.

Left: in 0 Gauge, Nigel Bowyers' Napier Street portrayed an urban goods yard in the Glasgow area in the 1950s.
(Photograph: Steve Flint)

Below left: Calderside, a 4mm Caledonian layout by the East of Scotland 4mm Group.
(Photograph: Alan Goodwillie)

Below: Grangetown, Trevor Hale originally built this early 1970s layout set to the East of Grangemouth on a line between Falkirk and Bo'ness. It is now owned by Tim Easter who runs more up to date stock, as seen here.
(Photograph: Tim Easter)

Left: today you can do your research aboard one of the new Class 334 units as seen here at Partick in 2005.

Below: and finally, I finish this chapter with another view on my original 4mm layout 'Lochside' this time with a trusty old Wrenn Class 20 taking to the stage.
(Photographs: the author)

purchased by a modeller who resides in East Lothian.

In 4mm scale at least, with the ever increasing availability of off-the-shelf diesel locos, coupled with advances in DCC and sound output, shed schemes are becoming increasingly popular with modellers. It is a genre ideal for the enthusiast with limited space in which to display a collection of traditionally Scottish types; and especially so, with the imminent release (at the time of writing) of the Heljan 26 and 27 classes.

The Central Belt can therefore provide modellers with much inspiration,

and particularly so, if your interest is not with small rural stations or Highland harbours! Though, notwithstanding the big city terminus schemes we considered earlier, the region does offer similar such prototypes in an urban or suburban setting. Further, as interest in post-steam modelling is increasing, they are particularly useful for modellers who prefer the era from the 1960s to present day. As would be expected, the 1960s period gives you more choice of motive power, including the classes 17, 20, 24, 25, 26, 27 and 21/29, and can still allow you to use the typical short-wheelbase vans and

wagons. However, history can be quite a strange affair to come to terms with, as some of the more modern privately-owned vehicles were starting to be utilised on freight workings during that period: I am thinking in particular of the tankers operated by the big oil companies and by chemical firms, and the BRT/Distillers grain hoppers.

In concluding this visit to the Central Belt: there's plenty of interest therefore in the region to satisfy most modellers and it is still possible to explore much of the system using the Strathclyde PT Zonecards or a First Scotrail Travelpass.

Some of these passes allow you to travel over their bus routes too, ensuring you can research those parts of the rail network which have lost their passenger services, or visit rail locations which are only served with freight. But they also enable you to soak up the atmosphere of urban Scottish Railways, which, I believe, is an essential prerequisite when it comes to creating authentic models and layouts back at home.

Chapter 6

From Fife to St Fillans

The Kingdom of Fife recalls days gone by when Scottish kings lived and hunted in the region, a peninsula which lies between the Firths of Forth and Tay. For the purpose of this chapter however, we shall encompass Fife itself and travel a little further west towards the Trossachs, and also northwards in order to include the many routes within Tayside.

The region is a halfway house between the densely populated lowland areas and the remoter and more rugged Highlands. From a modelling point of view, it really is an undiscovered gem of delightful prototypes just crying out to be modelled. Why the region has escaped the attentions of modellers for so long is a bit of a mystery, since it is abounds with all the hallmarks of classic railway modelling topics; from rural branch line terminii and industrial backwaters through to key main line routes and of course, the spectacular crossings of the mighty estuaries.

Fife itself was the birthplace of many ancient wagon-ways transporting coal down to the coasts. Wooden rails gave way to iron rails as the technology of the day improved and soon an impressive amount of mileage was in use. That was followed by the construction of an early main line route running across the region, south west to north east, linking Burntisland on the Firth of Forth with Craig on the south bank of the Firth of Tay. This location later became know as Tayport. At Ladybank, halfway along the route, a line headed off towards Perth. These lines were operating by the 1850s with a further connection added to Dunfermline. It was a clever scheme and soon became known as the Edinburgh, Perth and Dundee Railway, their main aim being to keep all of the territory to

Above: Burntisland station built by the East of Scotland 4mm Group is an example of pre-grouping NBR modelling at its best. This award winning P4 layout represents the year 1883, a period seldom modelled.

Left: This model of Kilconquhar on the Leven and East of Fife line was built by members of the NBRSG and depicts the station as it was during the First World War. *(Photographs: Allan Goodwillie)*

themselves. Ferries across the two Firths enabled the company to use the names of Edinburgh and Dundee in its title. It was to be quite a number of years before the great bridges across these wide estuaries were built.

What was even more interesting for the modeller, were the numerous branch lines which fanned away from these main routes, often built to serve more industries as well enabling the vast coal reserves of the area to be exploited. Thornton Junction developed as an important hub of lines radiating to Leven on the coast, and westward into the coalfield areas. A marshalling yard and locomotive shed were located here. Allan Goodwillie's 4mm layout Dubbieside (right) is an excellent example of a layout built to exemplify the type of traffic that just might have been around in the early days of British Railways.

Branch lines were built to Leslie and Auchmuty where a flourishing paper industry was to be found. Up until the early 1990s, a small branch west of Markinch (on the Dundee to Kirkcaldy line) was still in existence, serving several paper mills on the banks of the River Leven. The mills served included; the Balbirnie Mill, Rothes Paper Mill and the Auchmuty Mills. A fairly complex system of tracks were to be found, indeed they may still be in place today, though all of the traffic by rail had ceased by early 1990s. Coal for these mills came from the Bowhill Washery Plant near Cardenden in Fife.

The branch was steeply graded and for many years, indeed as far back as pre-grouping days, the old NBR J88 shunters were used. In later days BR Class 08 shunters were utilised whilst it is possible the mills themselves used small 'pugs' for their internal shunting. Most of the mills were taken over during the latter stages of the twentieth century and well known names such as Tullis Russell were to be found in that area. I have included a paper mill layout scheme (overleaf) inspired by the area and although designed with the distinctive private-owner clay hoppers of the Speedlink period in mind, it can be adapted to suit any period.

Near to Cowdenbeath and Dunfermline, there existed many colliery lines, some which lasted well into British

Top: Allan Goodwillie's Dubbieside layout captures the industrial side of Fife's railways in the 1950s. Coastal steamer 'James Gillies' awaits alongside the quay where a Class J83 is about to leave on a short goods train. In the background can be seen the coal hoists for the coal dock and funnels of other steamers waiting for bunkering. *(Photograph: Allan Goodwillie)*

Centre: the paper mills of central Fife are an obvious choice for modellers looking for an industrial theme. Here 08 515 is seen with a Tullis Russell clay hopper and a caustic soda tank on the Auchmuty Mills branch in 1986. *(Photograph: G. C. O'Hara)*

Right: rail served since pre-grouping days, they can be set in almost any period, like the Dalmore paper mill seen here c. 1935. *(Photograph: R. W. Lynn collection)*

DENNY PAPER MILL - A Lineside Industry Scheme

Many years ago I had an opportunity to visit a paper mill in the Denny area, close to Falkirk. There were quite a few mills in that area and some may still be in operation today. The highlight of the visit was to watch the paper making process from the start, then walking beside the plant to reach the end, where the paper was coming off the machine in a huge roll.

It was fascinating, at first I could only see water dropping between fine wires: mixed up with this water and hardly visible, was a fine pulp. The solution becomes more concentrated and it starts to form into the paper we know and use. It went through a number of processes, most of which I have forgotten, but I do remember it being dried: going up, down and over huge rollers as the moisture was taken out. The huge roll of finished paper was taken away ready for onward transportation. It was a noisy experience, and certainly a wet one; it was all witnessed over thirty years ago, so you can see what an impression it had on me.

The paper mill was also rail served and numerous vans were standing in sidings. I never saw any form of motive power in the mill itself, although I was informed they used to have their own steam locomotives, small 'Pugs' I believe. During my visit, a British Rail locomotive came into the complex to shunt vans and coal wagons as I recall.

If I remember correctly, the site was a mix of old stone buildings and large modern warehouse accommodation.

In 4mm, if structure modelling is not your thing, a quick way to source the industrial buildings would be to utilise many of the new card kits now becoming available from companies like Metcalfe Models. Certainly two kits in their range would be suitable; the brewery kit and the boilerhouse and factory kit. They also manufacture a bus garage, which no doubt could be adapted to look like a more modern unit. They would need to be built mainly as low relief structures, so some experience of 'card kitbashing' will be necessary. Barrels, kegs, tanks and crates from various sources, such as the

Ten Commandments range, would be required to detail the scene.

The scheme with associated sidings could either be a stand alone project, with simple hidden sidings at each end, or it could fill the corner of an existing layout. Whilst there would be the opportunity to run a shuttle style passenger train on the through line, the main thrust of this scheme is freight; though with plenty of interesting traffic potential. Raw materials inward would include china clay powder or slurry, esparto grass, chemical wood pulp, caustic soda and even rags. In earlier times, much of this would have arrived in drums or tanks loaded into standard vans or opens. In more recent times, and particularly in the Speedlink era, many specialist tank and hopper wagons were used.

The paper mill boilers were invariably powered by coal and that would require copious amounts to be delivered weekly, if not daily, by trip workings. The finished product would be taken away in box vans, or, in more modern times, the huge rolls would be loaded into VDA type vans and

Cargowaggons, or even sheeted into OBA wagons.

A suitable works locomotive would carry out all the internal shunting moves with BR locomotives shunting the exchange siding or loop.

Backdate the layout to the 1940s, and some suitable private owner coal wagons would add a splash of colour to the scene. Perhaps the paper mill had its own wagons, there are plenty of transfers or decals which allow you to manufacture a particular style, and those adept with a computer could have great fun designing their own.

The track plan is very suitable for adapting with extra loops or sidings, depending on your circumstances, and is not meant to tie anyone down to producing the exact configuration. It is more the principle of the paper mill idea, with its variety of traffic, that it exemplifies. We all use huge amounts of paper these days, and it is poignant to remember that it all starts from someone planting a little seedling, then waiting quite a number of years before it is ready to be sent to the mill to end up as paper.

Fife Paper Mill at a glance
Design scale: 4mm. **Location:** Central Fife. **Suggested period:** any, up to the 1980s. **Locomotive types:** various to suit chosen period, including industrial types. **Typical traffic:** coal, wood pulp, finished products outward.

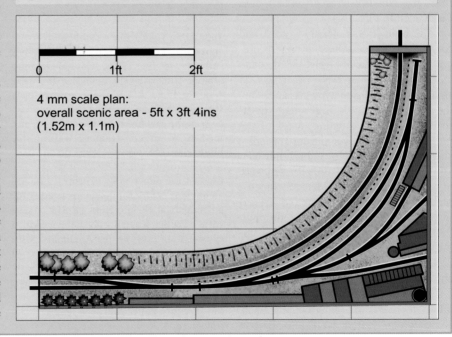

4 mm scale plan:
overall scenic area - 5ft x 3ft 4ins
(1.52m x 1.1m)

0   1ft   2ft

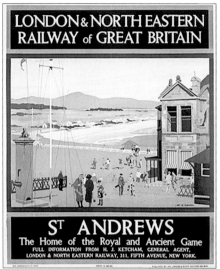

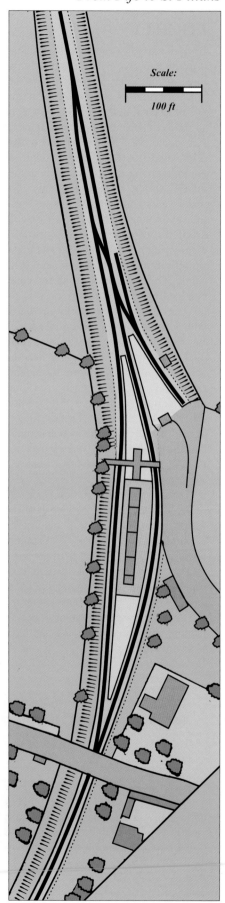

If ever there was a prototype station similar to some of my own layouts, it would have to be St Andrews: an island platform set in a shallow cutting (top) with just a loading dock siding and headshunt (centre). Very similar in fact to my Burnfoot scheme from the early 1980s. The goods yard at St Andrews was actually some 450 yards to the north of the station site, an ideal scenario if you just want to model a passenger station. The plan (right) shows the track layout c.1910, though it changed little, if at all, during its life.

(Photographs: R. W. Lynn collection)

Railways days. These had grown into quite large concerns covering substantial areas of land. There was a large group called the Elgin, Halbeath and Fordell Railway, which owned many mines and the associated mineral railways between them. As a measure of the importance the coal industry brought to the area, the whole class of LNER J38 0-6-0 locomotives (the forerunner of the more well-known J39) were to be found in the area. Kept at the locomotive sheds of Edinburgh (St Margarets), Dunfermline and Thornton Junction, their function was simply to serve the coal industry.

A similar undertaking at Wemyss (Fife), composing of numerous coal mines, operated its own private railway which took the black gold down to the harbour at Methil. Another familiar household product of yesteryear, linoleum floor covering (often known as 'Lino'), was produced in Kirkcaldy for many years and the North British Railway, who eventually, through a series of amalgamations, took over the smaller railway companies in the area, produced special lino wagons to transport the finished goods.

Much of the peninsula, especially in the east is rural. Eventually, a railway ran along the Fife coastline, reaching the University town of St Andrews, serving the many fishing villages along the way. Several very attractive stations existed on the route, all closed under Beeching.

LOCHTY

If your idea of a model railway is an 0-6-0 locomotive hauling and shunting three or four open wagons or vans, set in a very rural location, then the terminus of Lochty, at the end of fourteen or so miles of meandering single track in Fife could well be the answer. I first discovered this line from a couple of photographs in a book and was immediately struck by its simplicity. For many years I thought it consisted of a loop and a single siding. However, with a little bit of delving and the use of a magnifying glass I found an additional siding, if rather short, off the main siding. This very short siding served an end loading facility.

The line curved north-eastwards after leaving Leven, close to Thornton Junction and of course an area with docks and coalmines, before heading across the low hills and the formidable Largo Law (953ft). Opened in 1898 as the grandly sounding East Fife Central Railway, the line served this mainly agricultural area of Fife, which actually had the most stunning views over the Firth of Forth and across to Edinburgh. There had been one or two sidings serving some small coal mines along the route, one survived I believe into the 1940s, but the line was mainly an agricultural backwater. Passengers were never carried, except in the early 1900s, when some unadvertised coal miners' trains were operated. There were two or three stations along the line, but they were known as depots, a feature being that they did not have platforms of course.

Only three types of locomotive were allowed to operate the route (RA3); ex-NBR J35 and J36 0-6-0s, and N15, which were 0-6-2T locomotives. All three types were found at Thornton Junction (62A) but photographic evidence only exists for the two types of 0-6-0. Specimen numbers include J36 65345, which had a tender cab and was a regular performer on the line. A J35 No. 64488 was photographed at Largoward whilst I do have a photograph of N15 No. 69211 at Thornton Junction itself.

The terminus, or depot, at Lochty was extremely small, just right for a model layout, and the track plan must have changed little, if at all over the lines existence .The long siding had a brick loading dock and there was an old coach body raised off the ground near to the loop, this being the office from all accounts. The actual loop is quite short and could possibly hold no more than five or six wagons. I have reason to believe the track was still interlaced at closure. An old OS map shows the location of a crane, but I feel sure it had been removed shortly before the end. This occurred on 10 August 1964. There had been plans to extend the railway to St Andrews on the Fife coast, but this never happened. Being such a rural area, the authorities would

have decided possibly, that passenger receipts or indeed freight receipts would have not generated much more income. In any case, that delightful coastal route along the shores of the Firth of Forth already served the university town of St.Andrews.

The traffic was purely agricultural, as it was an important mixed farming area. There were arable and root crops as well as sheep and cattle. Potatoes and sugar beet were farmed each year and despite being of a seasonal nature, the traffic could be heavy. Most of the produce would utilise vans although sugar beet would frequently be taken out in sheeted wagons. There would have been the odd horse-box and cattle wagons on the line whilst incoming traffic would have included household coal, fertilizer, fodder and agricultural machinery would have also generated traffic. The latter would have arrived on special wagons such as low-loaders.

This small project must surely yearn to be modelled in one of the finer 4mm scales such as EM or P4, whilst it could also be considered for ScaleSeven or even S Gauge.

Nor would it look out of place in 2mm and 3mm scales either, requiring, as it does, only one or two locomotives and a modest handful of freight stock at the very most.

Lochty at a glance

Design scale: 4mm. **Location:** East Fife. **Suggested period:** 1950s - 1960s. **Locomotive types:** ex-NBR 0-6-0s, J35 or J36. **Typical traffic:** Freight only; mainly agricultural produce, coal.

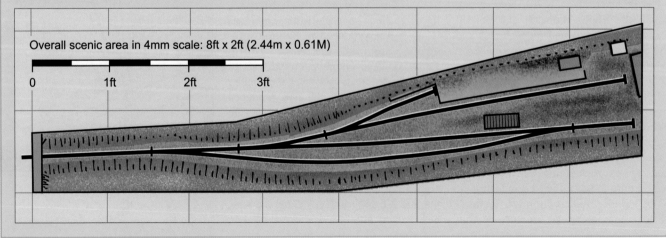

Overall scenic area in 4mm scale: 8ft x 2ft (2.44m x 0.61M)

0   1ft   2ft   3ft

The Lochty Branch Terminus

Below: the prototype showing its delightfully simplicistic layout, photographed in 1960 with a J36 shunting, and centre: my 1980s P4 layout Lochend that was based loosely on the track plan, though included a passenger platform which the original, as seen in the plan, left, did not have. *(Photographs: author and author's collection)*

Above: the track formation between the overbridges at the east end of Alloa station would surely lend itself to an interesting 'bitsa' station style layout. *(Photograph: Roy C. Crombie)*

Kilconquhar, illustrated on page 60 is a scale model of one of those stations. At another, Largo, the line ran across a short viaduct beneath which nestled a little harbour and collection of vernacular Fife cottages. The scenic element of any such layout would be the dominant modelling activity, especially appealing to the architectural modellers amongst us.

The traffic in the area was usually quite seasonal, with the potato and sugar beet crop requiring all sorts of open wagons and vans at different times of the year. One such line that meandered through the centre of Fife from Cameron Bridge to Lochty was built primarily for such traffic. It opened very late on, in 1893, and survived until 1964. The branch was more or less a freight line only, and the stations along the route were known as depots. Throughout its lifetime, it simply served the agricultural needs of this rural community. As the accompanying layout theme shows, the terminus at Lochty was a perfect example of a basic station or depot and was the inspiration behind 'Lochend', one of my early P4 layouts mentioned in chapter 1 and illustrated left.

To the west of Dunfermline, the North British operated a clutch of cross-country routes and short branch lines centred around Alloa and Stirling. The latter location of course, was firmly Caledonian territory and today, both of the main routes from Edinburgh and Glasgow meet a few miles south of the city. The North British entered Stirling from the east, via Alloa, which is another of those delightful country junction stations that has been completely overlooked by modellers. The main station itself is flanked at either end by road overbridges but the east end, beyond the station building and main overbridge, probably offers the most for an unusual modelling project. Here the Devon Valley line leaves the Dunfermline routes in a tight junction through a series of diamond crossings (left). The idea would be to model just the junction scene, with the main overbridge acting as the scenic break into a sector plate type fiddle yard. A challenging project for those who like building trackwork.

The branches around Alloa and its associated marshalling yard, including Alloa harbour branch, are very inspiring

and several small layouts have been constructed based on prototypes in the locality. Alloa Goods by Jeff Taylor (left) and Nigel Bowyer's classic Carron Road are two well known examples.

Most of the lines around Alloa lost their passenger services in the mid to late 1960s with passenger services to the town finally ceasing in 1968; some of these had been routed via the 'other' Forth Bridge at Throsk. Freight lingered on until 1983; however, today Alloa is much in the news, as there have long been plans afoot to create a new passenger service between Edinburgh and Stirling via the town. A certain amount of new trackwork would be required because some of it had been lifted when the freight services ceased.

To the west of Alloa there was the short branch to Alva. Closed to passengers as early as 1954, it retained freight, in the form of molasses tankers to a yeast factory, until the mid-1980s. There had also been a branch off this line, to a 1950s 'super pit' at Glenochil; although the pit never really fulfilled its potential, it presents another 'might have been' traffic source.

The route north-eastwards from Alloa was the picturesque Devon Valley line, which ran to Perth via Dollar, Rumbling Bridge and Kinross. There was another coal mine at Dollar and fairly heavy coal trains used the southern end of the route which kept that part of it open after the rest had closed under the Beeching axe. Perhaps the most attractive station was that at Rumbling Bridge: a perfectly laid out branch station for the modeller, complete with a road overbridge bridge to act as a scenic break at each end. This route is another one of Scotland's railways undiscovered gems and I include Rumbling Bridge as a potential layout scheme which would suit the early diesel modeller as well as the dyed-in-the-wool steam enthusiast.

Top: Jeff Taylor's EM gauge micro-layout 'Alloa Goods' sees a Clayton Type 1 (a detailed Tech-cad model by Peter Johnson) shunting the yard. *(Photograph: Steve Flint)*

Centre: A DMU stops at Rumbling Bridge in May 1964. *(Photograph: Douglas Hulme)*

Left: The up platform and shelter at Rumbling Bridge in 1951. D30 No 62441 heads a Stirling bound passenger train. *(Photograph: R. W. Lynn collection)*

RUMBLING BRIDGE

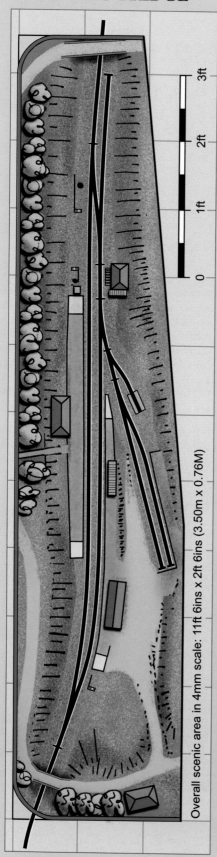

Overall scenic area in 4mm scale: 11ft 6ins x 2ft 6ins (3.50M x 0.76M)

The fourteen and a half mile Devon Valley line was opened throughout in 1871 although the section from Alloa to Tillicoultry was actually constructed by the Stirling and Dumfermline Railway. If ever a line was blessed with quirky sounding locations, it had to be the Devon Valley line with names like Tillicoultry, Dollar, Balado, Crook of Devon and of course Rumbling Bridge. Initially the NBR operated the line.

The line was a useful cross country branch serving its rural community in the picturesque valley for just over a hundred years. As mentioned in the main text, coal reserves kept the section between Alloa and Dollar, which was double track, open until 1973, but passenger services on the whole route had ceased in 1964. The section north from Dollar to Kinross, which was single track, then closed completely.

If ever a station was perfect for modellers, it has to be Rumbling Bridge: conveniently situated with a bridge at each end that is just perfect for taking the tracks off-stage. In 4mm scale, the station can be fitted into a length of 12ft - just slightly less than the prototypical scale length. Platforms were slightly staggered and the small goods yard had no goods shed. There was an unusual signal box built high into the embankment with result that the point rodding arrangements ran out over a wooden frame before turning through 90º over a selection of levers and pulleys which can just be seen in the lower photograph opposite.

There was a very short headshunt for the goods yard which included a loading bank with small crane and, between the wars, a spur for holding a platelayer's trolley. The station building was brick built to a standard design, whitewashed in part. A small shelter stood on the up platform.

On the station's southern approach there was a very tall NBR lattice post signal, located more or less next to the crossover leading into the goods yard. This signal did not have a ladder, it would have been a very scary job climbing up it in any case. Instead, the lamp was raised up and down the signal using a crank handle and pulley system - not an uncommon feature on ex-NBR lines. An old NBR coach body was found on the platform in use as a store. A set of wooden steps allowed access down the embankment onto the up platform, to the right of the shelter.

During the 1950s, there were six or seven trains daily each way and usually consisted of three or four coaches, some were through workings between Perth and Glasgow. Examples of both LNER and LMS stock have been recorded whilst the motive power was equally mixed. These ranged from elderly NBR or CR 0-6-0s and 4-4-0s to LNER K1s, K2s and K4s. Even the two V4 2-6-2s and the larger LNER B1 and LMS Black Fives were seen. Tank locomotives included the NBR C15s and C16s as well as LNER V1s and BR Standard Tanks. The smaller type NBR 0-6-0 tender locomotives would have been seen on daily goods service. Quite a variety on a small cross country line, and potential for operating in the green diesel period too.

Many of the above mentioned locomotive types are available in 4mm scale, and the NBR types in particular are also available as kits in 7mm scale. A 7mm BR Standard tank is planned to be released ready-to-run soon. Suitable coaching and freight stock is also readily available in both scales.

So, all in all an interesting passing station. My basic plan with two sets of hidden sidings would make a manageable project for one person in 4mm scale and could be the basis for a first move into EM or P4. The name of the layout alone would make an interesting talking point!

Rumbling Bridge at a glance
Design scale: 4mm. **Location:** Devon Valley Railway (Alloa and Kinross). **Suggested period:** BR steam/early diesel. **Locomotive types**: ex-NBR and CR types, BR Standards, Class 101 DMUs. **Typical traffic:** passenger, coal, cattle, agricultural produce and machinery.

To the west of Stirling, the North British and the Caledonian both possessed enclaves of territory in which each had a virtual monopoly. The North British encircled the Campsie Fells with a long branch via Bucklyvie, Gartness and eventually to Balloch, by the shores of Loch Lomond (along a short stretch of Caledonian and North British Joint). Off this route the NBR had its gateway into the Trossachs by means of a short branch to Aberfoyle. There was fierce competition between the two companies for the tourist traffic into the beautiful Trossachs locality. The Caledonian had its own route into the Trossachs, branching of its main line to Perth at Dunblane. The line passed through Callander, en-route to Oban on the west coast. Originally built by the Callander and Oban Railway, of which more later, it ran through the Pass of Leny and along the shore of Loch Lubnaig before heading off towards Oban at Balquidder Junction. The tourist focal point in the Trossachs is, of course, Loch Katrine where steamers still operate to this day from a pier at the eastern end of the loch. It is a beguiling and enchant-

Above: akin to a light railway terminus the ex-NBR station at Aberfoyle became a rather ramshackle affair, the goods shed in particular looked as if it could have collapsed at any time. A magical prototype however, full of atmosphere and crying out to be modelled: seen here in 1954. *(Photograph: R. W. Lynn collection)*

ing place, surrounded by steep, tree-clad hillsides. One where a little imagination and modellers' licence could quite easily give rise to scenarios of either the NBR's Aberfoyle branch being extended, or the CR building a branch from Callander to

Loch Katrine pier head. Either way, it would make an attractive might-have-been layout featuring a pier and steam ship set amidst a rugged landscape and incorporating passenger excursions with some minimal freight, such as coal for the steamer. Perhaps as epitomised by the accompanying watercolour.

The Caledonian Railway objected strongly to the interference of the North British in areas where it felt it was the major company. Its branch heading west to Oban has already been mentioned with the section from Dunblane being an important tourist route for the company once it had taken over the local concern running the line. The two companies met again at Crianlarich, although very little interchange of traffic took place even after Nationalisation in 1947. The Caledonian line remained the main route into Oban until the section between Crianlarich and Callander closed in 1965

following a landslide in Glen Ogle; although comprising of simply a few small rocks, closure had in any case been approved already. Trains to Oban were then directed from Glasgow up the West Highland line to use the connecting tracks at Crianlarich to reach the Oban line proper. Even today, by all accounts, you do not tell the Oban drivers that they are working on the 'branch'!

The route off the Oban line at Balquidder Junction ran east to Perth via Lochearnhead, St Fillans and Crieff, with a further branch between Crieff and Gleneagles. Again, these attractive stations have been completely overlooked by modellers - maybe because most of these lines lost their passenger services in the mid 1960s and few photographs seem to have survived, or have yet to be discovered. The Crieff to Perth section actually lost its passenger service as early as 1951 and the small branch off this

route, to Methven, closed to passengers in 1937, reminding us that both the LMS and LNER did close lines to passengers as early as the 1930s. The infamous Dr Beeching cannot be blamed all of the time for his pruning of the network during the 1960s. The accountants in London really did keep a close eye on the passenger receipts and would take action if need be to keep the costs down, and not just in Scotland. One wonders if local residents in the 1930s really did have a voice when it came to their local station or line being closed. After all, car ownership did not catch on until after the Second World War. In its final days, the dying ember of the Crieff route was serviced by examples of the 4 wheel railbuses in a vain attempt to keep the route viable.

Just as an aside but relevant here, one must not forget the charming Aberfeldy branch close by. It was off the Highland

Some larger stations worth modelling

Left: Callander prospered as a Victorian Spa town and the railway arrived in 1858, later becoming part of the Caledonian route through to Oban. The passenger station, with its grand timber buildings, was built about half a mile to the west of the goods yard, so a layout featuring both would be a large affair, possibly built along opposite walls in a dedicated railway room. This view shows an ex-LMS 2-6-4T No. 42199 with a train for Stirling in 1954. *(Photograph: W. A. C. Smith)*

Below: Crieff is the second largest town in Perthshire but lost its substantial railway facilities in the 1960s. The spacious goods yard is shown below left c. 1960 *(Photograph: WFRM collection)* **whilst the passenger facilities, below right, sees 45016 with a train for Gleneagles in 1955.** *(Photograph: W. A. C. Smith)*

main line just north of Perth and Stanley Junction, leaving at Ballinluig and following the River Tay. It had just one intermediate stop at Grandtully before arriving at yet another attractive Scottish terminus. Aberfeldy has been the subject of at least one layout I am aware of in the past, but for those modellers who enjoy the might-have-been style of layout, it had been hoped that the branch could have been extended about six miles further down the valley to the shores of Loch Tay itself. As mentioned elsewhere, there was already a short branch to Killin at the other end of Loch Tay, and I do believe the idea was to operate a steamer service on the loch linking the two railways. It was naturally a local concern but, as usual in such cases, the funding was not available, so it never came about. Nevertheless, it provides a similar

scheme to that suggested for Loch Katrine above, though in this case it would eventually have been a Highland Railway branch. A worked example of the idea, called 'Kenmore', was once modelled in N Gauge by Peter Fletcher.

The Aberfeldy branch passenger service was operated for many years by a Caledonian 439 Class 0-4-4T locomotive and a couple of ancient LMS coaches, with the service often running as a mixed train, as above. The Aberfeldy branch closed to passenger traffic in May 1965, with the freight traffic strangely ceasing two months earlier. In its final days a single passenger coach was often seen in the charge of a Class 24 or 26 diesel.

Included in this chapter and region are the great cities of Perth and Dundee, the area around the Sidlaw Hills and part of the old county of Angus. East of Perth,

towards the Dundee area, the Caledonian Railway had numerous routes including its main line to Aberdeen from Stanley Junction via Forfar. This route, which eventually closed in 1967 (though freight traffic lingered from Stanley Junction to Forfar until 1982) had an assortment of small branch lines heading into the area known as Strathmore. A well-known example, the branch to Bankfoot, lost its passenger service in 1931 but relied on potato traffic until 1964. It was a typical rural terminus, with run round facilities by the platform, a small goods yard complete with wooden goods shed and a few sidings for storage.

Next was a short branch from Coupar Angus on the main line to Blairgowrie, which managed to hang onto its passenger service until 1955 and its freight service for another ten years or so. If my memory serves me right, I remember seeing an early P4/S4 layout of this delightful terminus, which was adorned with a superb overall roof. From Alyth Junction, a small branch to the cramped terminus of Alyth itself headed northwards, whilst southwards, the Caledonian had a further route into Dundee. Yet another small branch headed into Kirriemuir, losing its passenger service in 1952 but keeping freight until 1965, the same year that the Alyth branch closed completely. The route also linked into Arbroath and Montrose where the current main line runs to Aberdeen. This route was originally the Dundee and Arbroath Joint Railway but the North British used it to reach Montrose and also worked a branch line along the coast to Bervie. The abandoned route of this delightful little branch can still be followed if you leave the main A90 trunk road, and follow the coast road. There where several stations along this little branch and one, St Cyrus, a sure-fire candidate for a small layout project, is detailed opposite.

Above: eminently modellable were the mixed passenger and goods trains common to many Scottish branch lines. Here one arrives at Aberfeldy in 1959, headed by an ex-CR McIntosh 0-4-4T No. 55200.
(Photograph: D. H. Beecroft/Colourail)

Left: St Cyrus station on the Inverbervie branch seen in 1938 with an example of the smaller ex-CR McIntosh 0-4-4T, No. 9475.
(Photograph: R. W. Lynn collection)

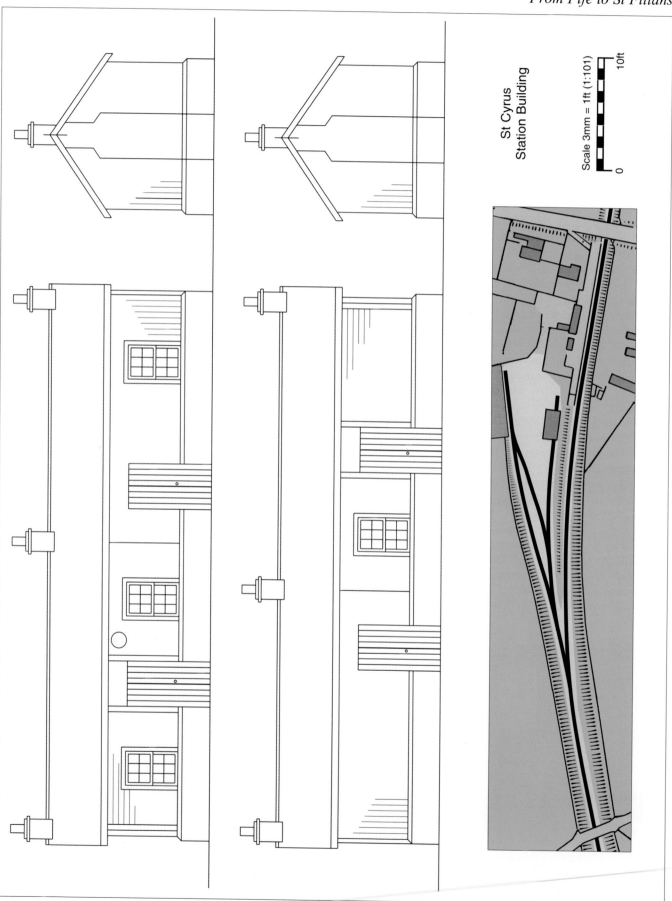

St Cyrus
Station Building

Scale 3mm = 1ft (1:101)

0   10ft

Moving away from bucolic branch themes for a while, Scotland's third city, Dundee, had been a port since medieval times and became an important railway centre in its own right. The linen and jute industry were well established with flax being imported from the Baltic ports. Shipbuilding and engineering were also important, whilst food processing has resulted in many famous brands being introduced from within the city. A thriving publishing firm; D.C. Thompson and Co. Ltd., who brought us characters like Oor Wullie, Dennis the Menace and Minnie the Minx, still operate in Dundee today. The city originally had terminus stations, at Dundee (East) and Dundee (West), and through stations at Dundee Tay Bridge and Maryfield. The terminus at Dundee (East) would be a good example for modellers to study with its fine overall roof and quite narrow platforms. Today there is only one station in Dundee - Tay Bridge - with a rather dark and cramped island platform surrounded by tall retaining walls.

There had always been extensive sidings in and around the station area, as well as a branch to the adjacent harbour, and I remember making a special visit many years ago to view the locomotive depot and yard and record on film the last of the small Barclay Class 06 shunting locomotives. I managed to obtain some excellent black and white photographs on that April day in 1978 including 06 002 seen below. Whilst on the depot, I took photographs of the inevitable Class 27 locomotives, as well as a Class 122

(Photograph: courtesy GNSRA)

'bubble car'. From that photograph, I now realise that I painted my own 7mm model in the wrong livery for the period!

Dundee as a modelling topic, whether one or other of the original terminus stations, closed c. 1959/60, or today's current station, would be a major undertaking, but parts of the network could be singled out for a project, such as the harbour branch for instance, where small locomotive types and sharp radius curves abounded. Indeed, in many of the goods yards in Scotland, Dundee included, and in particular around dock areas, locomotives had to deal with quite tightly curved trackwork. During steam operation the various companies constructed small 0-4-0 tank locomotives to meet these circumstances. The NBR had the tiny Y9 engines, which used to haul their coal supply around with them on a small four-wheeled truck. The GNoSR had an equally small Z4 locomotive with an 0-4-2 wheel arrangement (above) and the Caledonian also had a small 0-4-0T. The generic term of 'Pug' for such locos is very much associated with Scottish railway vernacular. The LMS introduced a small dock shunting 0-6-0T designed by H. Fowler and five of these locomotives were found in Scotland, mainly in the Central Belt.

It became necessary to replace such small wheel-based steam engines

with similar small diesel classes when steam was phased out. In 1953 the North British Locomotive Company of Glasgow produced two batches of 0-4-0 diesel hydraulic locomotives with a six-foot wheelbase for BR. The first batch, Nos 11700 - 11702 (D2700-D2702) were a distinctive design, used in outside industry, with a little 'bunker' behind the cab. Despite the order originating from a Scottish Region requirement, these locos spent most of their lives away from their Scottish birthplace, on the Goole harbour network. The second batch though, numbered 11703 –11707 (D2703 - D2707) were allocated to Scottish depots. In 1957, a further group of 0-4-0 locomotives with a much better designed cab were delivered to Scottish Region from the NBL Co. The first dozen were numbered 11708 – 11719 (later D2708-19) with a second batch being delivered after the change in numbering system, as D2720-80. Whilst they were ideal for operating in the yards and on trip workings, they had a very short life as their natural habitat was fast disappearing and the 1960s National Traction Plan called for a reduction of the fleet size, in particular non-standard locomotives: the two types were mostly withdrawn during 1967 and 1968.

When you consider how long their predecessors had been in service, it seems quite a disgrace. However, in 1958 another class of 0-4-0s were introduced which soon become much more synonymous with Scottish shunting and

(Photograph: the author)

trip operation: the shunters produced by the Andrew Barclay Company of Kilmarnock. These, as I have mentioned before, eventually became the TOPS Class 06. Whilst again, some were withdrawn as early as 1967, a few 06s actually survived until the early 1980s in places where the larger 08s could not be used. Incidently, modellers should take note that the 0-6-0 Gardner-engined shunter classes; 03 and 04: which were so well-known elsewhere and epitomised by the 4mm Bachmann model: were not used in Scotland. However, the stylised Hunslet built 05s were very similar mechanically, and were seen at Thornton and Dunfermline sheds, amongst others.

This little episode regarding diminutive diesel shunters is perhaps slightly out of place here, but the recollections of looking for them during the 1960s and 70s is a very strong memory for me and publication of the photographs I took of them brought me my very first brush with the Tax Office over fees received! The point however is that they make interesting and ideal motive power for small layouts featuring shunting yards, loco stabling points, dockside branches, and the like. Various 4mm and 7mm etched kits are available for the 06 locomotive, whilst the Hornby model can be modified to make a reasonable example of this very useful locomotive. Further, the early type of NBL Co. Ltd 0-4-0 shunters and the Hunslet 05 are available as kits in 4mm scale from Judith Edge Kits range.

This region is an excellent area to research for modelling and one which in my opinion is much undervalued by layout builders. If you have an interest in small steam operated layouts and especially the Caledonian or North British Railway, this region is worth considering. However, do not discount the early diesel scene of the 1950s and 1960s. Many passenger routes in the region became operated by two-car DMUs, whilst a few of them were host to the early single-car 'Railbuses' as they were tried out up and down the country. Alas, vast tracts of these railway routes have been lost to the motor car and omnibus. It is thus up to modellers and layout builders to recreate these marvels of the past in miniature and preserve a little of the magic and romance that is lost forever.

Scottish Diesel Shunter Types

Some characteristic 1960s Scottish diesel shunter types modelled in EM gauge by Peter Johnson. Above: Hunslet Class 05 D2595, an adaptation of an A1 Models kit with a 'cut-and-shut' cab conversion to create the taller type fitted to later locos.

Barclay Class 06 D2444 is scratchbuilt in Plastikard, on a Branchlines chassis kit. and powered by a Portescap motor/gearbox. A spare door from another loco has supposedly been fitted at some point, hence the duplicated BR totems.

The little NBL, D2704, a very heavy adaptation of an old Playcraft item. Although a basic model from the 1960s, it catches the look very well, running on a DJH Class 02 chassis. All these types are now available in the Judith Edge range of kits.

Chapter 7

North by North West

Perhaps the most inspiring area of Scotland with regards to scenic beauty is that which encompasses the Far North and the Western Highlands. What is also perhaps the greatest British railway wonder of the 21st century is that most of the lines built in this region survive to this day for the enjoyment and delight of everyone, untouched almost by that most notorious railway hatchet-man: Doctor Beeching. I refer of course to the lines to Wick and Thurso and the ports serving the Western Isles; Kyle of Lochalsh, Mallaig, Fort William and Oban. These lines have given modellers much inspiration over the years. That they are some of the most scenic lines in Britain is not in dispute, their history has been written about frequently, and there are countless videos and DVDs extolling their magnificence. By their very nature they were built through difficult territory and sparsely populated landscape, the probability of large profits for the shareholders of the companies who proposed and built the lines, must have been extremely thin. It was only at the turn of the nineteenth and twentieth centuries did the Governments of the day decide that some financial initiatives should be provided to assist these companies. Some of the lines were built in opposition to nearby companies, as they grappled with the need to extend or defend their territory, and in the end three of the Scottish pre-grouping companies owned routes in the area under discussion.

Above: this region is ideal for creating small branch line layouts that still had a lot of pre-grouping architecture around as late as the 1970s, as illustrated on Loch Lochy. *(Photograph: Steve Flint)*

Below: in contrast I chose a 1950s steam theme on St Catherine's for Loch Fyne, though with a few alterations it could be transformed easily to another period - diesel or pre-grouping, whatever your preference. *(Photograph: the author)*

Above: much of this region was Highland Railway territory, a fiercly independant concern that was one of the first companies to use the larger 4-6-0 locomotives, such as the Jones Goods as seen on Peter Fletcher's EM gauge Far North layout 'Ardbealach'.

Right: the station at Ardbealach showing all the trappings of the Highland Railway scene just prior to the grouping in 1922. The building is based on that at Rogart.
(Photographs: Steve Flint)

Starting in the north, the Highland Railway had long established itself as the only company north of its headquarters in Inverness. True, the Great North of Scotland Railway with its headquarters in Aberdeen did indeed attempt to make forays into Highland territory, but these were safely resisted. Geographically, the routes chosen to head north were obstructed by vast expanses of water in the form of the Beauly Firth and Cromarty Firth. Further north again is Dornoch Firth. Consequently, any routes northwards could never be direct, and as a result, mileages were much longer than as the crow flies. Nevertheless, a line was built from Inverness to Dingwall, opening in 1862. It was then proposed to go further north to Invergordan and Tain, that part of the route opened a year later in 1863. The next section to Bonar Bridge was opened late in 1864 and then to Brora, completing the circumnaviga-tion of the Dornoch Firth via Lairg.

From here northwards, it needs to be mentioned that the next sections of the railway were constructed privately with much funding by the Duke of Sutherland. He contributed to the company allowing it to extend the line along the coast to Helmsdale, a very beautiful stretch of line by the way. It was now 1870, and two years later the Highland Railway took over the control of the lines north of Inverness.

In the very north there are only two main centres of population; Wick and Thurso. A railway, the Sutherland & Caithness Railway was built between the two towns whilst at the same time the line north from Helmsdale was to head inland and traverse the moors to reach the Wick and Thurso line at Georgemas Junction, the most northerly junction in Britain and the subject of one of my smallest layout themes in this book, in the adjacent panel. All of this took place by 1874 when the Far North link was completed. Much later by 1902, a few branch lines, all with modelling potential, had appeared, including a small light

GEORGEMAS JUNCTION

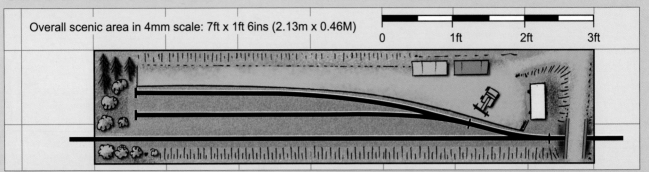

Overall scenic area in 4mm scale: 7ft x 1ft 6ins (2.13m x 0.46M)

0   1ft   2ft   3ft

This design is a bit of a cheat really! That is, because it is not a complete layout representing the most northerly junction on the network, only part of it, and not even the junction itself. As a result, it could be anywhere on the modern Scottish network. It has been designed yet again for modellers who are starved of space, and only have a few feet or a metre or two available. The whole layout could simply fold away and be stored in a cupboard. I believe this type of layout is nowadays called a 'Micro-Layout'.

I first noticed the possibility of such a scheme on a recent trip up the Far North line. The DMU had sped along to Thurso, and was now heading back to Georgemas Junction in order to end its journey at that other splendid terminus, Wick. As I passed, I caught a glimpse of an EWS liveried locomotive in the loop at Georgemas Junction with a short train of container flats. It was the

Below: the 'Safeway Flyer' brought big locomotives to a set of very small sidings. 37 503 and 37 674 were spotted on 21st April 2000, though Class 66s were also commonplace. The theme could readily be replicated anywhere in Scotland.
(Photograph: Grahame Elgar)

'Safeway Flyer' with produce for the then local Safeway stores. As my train pulled away from Georgemas for Wick, it passed under a road bridge and on the right hand side of my carriage two sidings came into view. Unfortunately I was unable to see whether they were connected via the main running line or the loop?

The sidings were surrounded by a large concrete standing area with one or two Safeway containers dotted about and a small Portacabin. Stationary at the end of the sidings were some VGA vans. The only other item of note was a large tractor unit which was used to load and unload the container flats. The Continental model firm Kibri make a HO version of this vehicle which is quite suitable for 4mm layouts.

Such a similar scene could easily be modelled in a small space allowing you to make use of the Bachmann intermodal wagons and some modern

motive power. If a small set of hidden sidings were at one end, and you modelled the main line to Wick, the DMU could run back and forwards in between the shunting operations. All it would require is a few yards of track and a couple of turnouts. It would possibly only need a single feed and return for the power, but again, such a small project could see the start of a DCC controlled layout without too much financial outlay. Of course, there is nothing to stop you modelling the full Georgemas Junction although these small 'cut-off' layouts can make interesting but quick-to-complete projects.

I have always fancied modelling Scotsgap Junction in this way, but only the part west of the road bridge. There would be three turnouts, a small turntable and the opportunity to operate two branch lines via a set of hidden sidings, on the station side of the road bridge. Just a thought...!

Georgemas at a glance

Design scale: 4mm, envisaged as a 'shelf' layout with a small fiddle yard at each end that fold up for storage. **Location:** Far North line, but the concept can easily be located elsewhere. **Suggested period:** present day. **Locomotive types:** Class 37, 66, 67, 158. **Typical traffic:** containers, intermodals, gas pipes.

The 'Far North' Line.

This route from Dingwall to Wick and Thurso possesses a number of attractive stations, all worth modelling and some relatively unchanged even after the arrival of Class 156 DMUs and modern signalling systems in the late 1980s.

Right: Helmsdale in 1980, set against the beautiful backdrop of the Strath of Kildonan. It is a larger passing station that had a steam sub-shed and turntable until the 1960s.

Below left: Forsinard is a little oasis in a moorland wilderness. Mainly a crossing place, it had a simple goods yard with small shed. One siding is still retained today for PW purposes.

Below right: the train shed at Wick still survives in its original form (as does that at Thurso) and despite the modern adornments, it is still an attractive modelling proposition.

(Photographs: the author. Helmsdale, Steve Flint)

railway built to Dornoch from the Mound, a quaint junction station on the Far North line. A further light railway opened from Wick to Lybster in 1903, financed in part by a Treasury grant.

Just a few yards north of Dingwall, a line westwards to Kyle of Lochalsh was proposed: the Dingwall and Skye line: it was started in the 1860s but not fully opened until 1897. The route was beset with financial problems and took many years to reach its destination. For quite a long period the terminus of the line was at Strome Ferry, beautifully situated at the very edge of Loch Carron and opened in 1870. Strangely enough, the Caledonian invested money in the line. Another branch from Fodderty Junction was built to the spa town of Strathpeffer, again a lovely station to model and I'm still amazed that I've not seen one yet. A typical branch terminus if ever there was one with a stylish platform canopy that is still extant to this day.

The line to Kyle of Lochalsh passes through some of the most beautiful but sparsely populated countryside in the UK. The romance of being hauled by an ex-Highland Railway locomotive or a Black Five engine of the LMS is now long gone, and even the joy of being behind a Class 26 or 37 diesel locomotive is now but a memory, though the Class 158 DMUs seem to cope with the tough gradients and winding curves, and of course, the magnificent scenery never seems to change.

Freight opportunities for the modeller on the Far North and Kyle lines are not in abundance, though historically there was plenty; fish, coal, livestock, general merchandise, parcels and newspapers were the main traffics, peat and timber were moved in quantities also. During the two World Wars, the lines were very busy ferrying troops, munitions and stores which were then sent to the fleets at Scapa Flow. For a short period in the mid-1970s, North Sea oil exploration platforms were built at Loch Kishorn close to Strome Ferry, bringing a daily train of construction materials, including cement and fly-ash in 'Presflo' wagons. In recent years on the Far North route

timber has been removed from Kinbrace and further deforestation will occur over the next few years, though the timber, as it happens, is of a very poor quality due in some instances to the climate and soil.

Oil trains still run up to Lairg with domestic coal being sent to Wick and Thurso. The aforementioned Safeway container trains, the source of inspiration for the Georgemas Junction scheme, ran for a few years but are not operating at present. Gas and oil pipe trains have operated to the sidings as well.

Along the full route there are plenty of small passing stations to observe and the modelling opportunities are varied. A particular favourite is the passing station at Forsinard, at the head of Strathalladale. Opened by the Sutherland and Caithness Railway in 1874, and upgraded by the Highland Railway, it is still a little green oasis amidst the stark and lonely Flow Country of northern Scotland. The original S&C station building is still standing and could be adopted for a fictional scheme if desired.

However, from a modelling point of

view, it is not just the lines that the Highland Railway actually built that need to be considered. It is the numerous proposed schemes in the region that were never built, that would make fine projects to model. Within a period of thirty years between the 1890s and the 1920s, a commission in conjunction with the HR looked, more than once, at particular areas likely to benefit from rail connections. Eventually some Acts of Parliament were obtained, but the usual problems of finance ensured that the lines were never completed. A branch from Garve to Ullapool featured high on the list of proposals, further down the Kyle line, a line from Achnasheen to Aultbea was identified, whilst from the Far North route, long branches were proposed from Culrain to Lochinver via Oykell Bridge and Lairg to Laxford Bridge. A line directly north from Forsinard to Port Skerra was actually authorised but lack of finance again halted construction.

There were other routes in the Wick and Thurso areas considered, to Scrabster and Dunnet, whilst an extension southwards from Lybster was also thought viable. Further south, additional lines to Cromarty and Portmahomack, both on peninsulas, were mentioned. The Highland Railway had hoped the Government of the day would assist with finance, but this did not happen, other than in a couple of cases, one example being the extension to the Kyle line.

Ideas aplenty for modellers who prefer the 'might have been' scenario, and indeed some modellers have already been there with their own interpretations of Highland branches. Dave Walker built the Laxford Bridge branch in 0 Gauge back in the early 1980s, whilst my publisher's representative, Steve Flint, constructed a small 4mm layout based on a possible line to the Kyle of Tongue, although that was not actually a destination considered by the Highland. Nigel Bowyer built another 4mm layout based on the proposed extension from Lybster to Dunbeath on the east coast, and there have been numerous other interpretations to places such as Lochinver and Ullapool. Whilst modelling layouts that might-have-been is sometimes not taken seriously by established exponents in the hobby, I believe it is very rewarding: the choice of buildings, rolling stock and signalling is made that much easier because, invariably, the 'house style' of the company represented is established and one's modelling purchases relating to the locos and rolling stock can be targeted accordingly. It is with this philosophy in mind that I include Ullapool as a modelling project in the adjacent panel.

Some examples of the Highland Railway's terminus stations that might-have-been; Adrian Walby's 'Lochinver' (above) and Steve Flint's Kyle of Tongue (left). Both were set in the 1970s when BRCW Sulzer Type 2s were the mainstay motive power and mixed passenger and goods trains were still operated under BR.
(Photographs: Steve Flint)

Above right: not Ullapool at all, but Laxford Bridge, another of the proposed HR branches that didn't materialise. This one was built in 0 gauge in 1980 by Dave Walker and gives us an insight into how such pre-grouping branch lines might have looked. *(Photograph: Brian Monaghan)*

ULLAPOOL

The Highlands of Scotland are well known for their sparse population but stunning and beautiful rugged scenery. The west coast in particular has a number of compact harbours around which small isolated settlements grew up. They relied mainly upon fishing and farming for their livelihoods until perhaps the Victorian era, when tourism became an issue, first of all with the rich, and then with the coming of the railways, the working classes. Unfortunately, the small settlements spread out along the west coast were too far away from many of the railways lines, but that did not stop some of the companies proposing routes to them.

As mentioned in the main text the Highland Railway postulated quite a number of schemes in North West Scotland. These schemes make what I call 'just supposing' layouts: a term borrowed from LMS modeller Arthur Whitehead by the way. Ullapool, with its land-locked harbour and one time herring fishing stronghold, was one such destination. It was also the nearest port to the Isle of Lewis with steamer connections to Stornaway. Garve, about 32 miles away was the nearest railhead on the Kyle of Lochalsh line.

A railway was actually planned and authorised in August 1890 and the HR was to work the line. Unfortunately, the company could not raise the necessary capital and despite the GNoSR coming

along in 1892 with offers to assist, the whole scheme eventually floundered. Other actual schemes similar to the Ullapool Railway are mentioned in the main text, but a look along the coastline of the region will introduce you to many other little settlements with equally intriguing place names.

Ullapool nowadays is quite a centre for tourism, quite a way off the beaten track, but what a different place it perhaps would have been if the railway had reached it. It would have a modest track plan, single platform with a run-round facility, and two or three sidings. In steam days there would have been a small engine shed with an equally small turntable, large enough to turn a Highland 'Loch' or 'Ben'. No doubt the

engine shed would still offer a little bit of shelter to a Class 24 or Class 26 during the early diesel days.

As drawn it is intended for 4mm scale steam operation, in whatever period suits. Pre-grouping would be interesting though many Highland locomotive types survived: during the LMS period they were particularly handsome in the LMS red/crimson livery of the day, and several made it through to BR days. For these periods, sourcing available kits and scratch-building the stock would be necessary. However, move to the 1950s and '60s, and there are several ready-to-run locomotives, such as the Hornby Black 5, that were frequently seen running on ex-Highland lines.

The plan can be adapted to N gauge, certainly for modern times using RTR Class 158s with Class 66s on timber or container trains, though, naturally some of the sidings would have gone, along with the older buildings.

Ullapool at a glance

Design Scale; 4mm. **Location:** North West Coast. **Suggested period:** steam, suitable any period, from pre-grouping to the 1950s. **Locomotive types:** see text. **Typical traffic:** passenger, general merchandise, parcels, timber, quarried stone, fish, fuel oil.

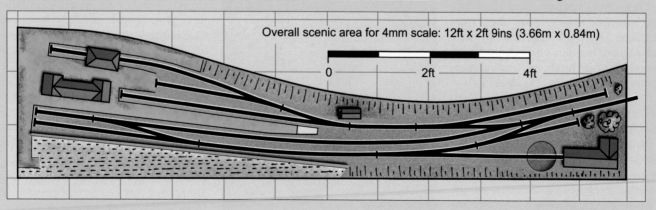

Overall scenic area for 4mm scale: 12ft x 2ft 9ins (3.66m x 0.84m)

0   2ft   4ft

Right: Loch Awe station on the Oban route was squeezed between a rocky backdrop and the shoreline of the Loch. A suitable prototype thus, for a shelf-style baseboard. *(Photograph: Douglas Hulme)*

Many of the lines in the Highlands, especially at the end of the 19th century and also in the early part of the 20th century, were actually constructed for social reasons with, as mentioned previously, occasional aid of Treasury finance. It was acknowledged that vast tracts of the Highlands were at a disadvantage and there was indeed much rural poverty. The pre-grouping companies of the time simply wanted to avoid competition with the other companies and provide worthwhile revenues from passengers and such freight as there was. General merchandise, coal, fish and timber provided the early companies with freight. Other industries arrived in the Highlands: paper making and aluminium smelting being some of the largest, they relied on huge amounts of water for their production, so the Highlands were a most suitable location, but the impact of them was not felt until much later. These examples provide modellers of more modern periods the opportunity to have specialist traffic flows, such as those identified in chapter 5, page 51, and centred around the Mossend Speedlink services. I refer here to china clay, wood pulp and alumina inwards, with finished products outwards. Some of these specialist traffics are just still with us today, although they remain quite vulnerable to economic markets and the whims of the private companies operating the services.

Moving now to the south west of this region, the celebrated 'Rails to the Isles' were built through to the west coast and two still survive, although one of them has been much cut back. Nowadays they are marketed together as the 'West Highland Lines' to Oban, Fort William, and Mallaig but they commenced life as two independent routes by two rival companies as we examined in chapter 2.

A route to Oban had been considered as far back as 1845 and eventually the railway managed to reach as far as Callander in 1858 and Glenoglehead in 1870, but the remainder of the original route was abandoned. However, the Caledonian Railway, along with the LNWR, eventually provided finance for

the rest of the route and it opened in stages through to Oban by 1880. It had not been an easy line to construct and quite naturally not all the railway navvies working on the line preferred the harsh winter climate of the Highlands!

From Glenoglehead the C&O threaded through Glen Dochart to reach Crianlarich where it would later be crossed at high level by the West Highland Railway. The WHR station at Crianlarich is perhaps the better known of the two, with its celebrated platform cafe, and has certainly been the subject of modelling interpretations in the past. After nationalisation, the spur between the two lines was utilised totally, once the Dunblane - Callander - Crainlarich section closed prematurely, due to a punitive landslide in 1965.

From here, the C&O continued westwards through Strathfillan and Glen Lochy to Dalmally and Loch Awe

(above), another delightful lochside station that cries out to be modelled. The line ran through the Pass of Brander, where because of the danger of falling boulders, a special signalling system was provided. Then on through Taynuilt and Connell to Oban itself. In similar vein to the north west Sutherland region of Scotland, this region also has vast tracts of land into which railways could have been built. In particular the Corran and Kintyre peninsulas, both full of settlements that could with modeller's license have been possible destinations. Inverary and Dunoon spring to mind, along with Lochgilphead at the western end of the Crinan canal. Even Campbeltown could be a possible destination in standard gauge, if not in narrow gauge: it was of course home to the short lived Campbeltown and Machrihanish 2ft 3ins gauge line, built principally to outship coal from the Machrihanish mine and modelled many years ago by Nigel Macmillan.

The area is much less rugged, indeed almost pastoral, than the Highland regions and layouts would thus reflect this. Most would probably have been Caledonian Railway branches, but even the WHR/NBR could have penetrated the region: my layout St Catherines for Loch Fyne, pictured above right (see also pages 12 and 74) being one such projection from Arrochar and Tarbet.

As I examined in chapter 2, the proposed Glasgow and North Western

Left: A re-engined NBL Class 29 built by Peter Johnson, guests on 'Dalmally' Paul Timperley's EM Gauge ex-Callander and Oban layout. *(Photograph: Steve Flint)*

Railway had hoped to pass through Fort William, had it been successful in gaining Royal Assent and the necessary funding. In the end the G&NWR proposal was defeated, though residents of the Fort William area in particular were very keen to have a railway. In 1889 the original project was revised with a slightly different route entering Fort William from the east and the Spean Valley. A small two-mile branch was also part of the proposal, to run from Spean Bridge to a station by Loch Lochy in the Great Glen itself. This section was actually withdrawn before the act was passed, in order to calm the Highland Railways fears, but it didn't stop me from constructing the station as it might have been in the 1970s. The layout, which at the time of writing is my current project and for the purposes of this book I was persuaded by my publisher to present it for a few photographs in 1950s guise: hence the picture right, and the front cover!

Before leaving the Oban route I want to return briefly to Glenoglehead, where a small branch, which has been the inspiration for many modellers, was constructed to the nearby village of Killin from a new station on the main route at Killin Junction. The branch itself opened in 1886, having a terminus station with locomotive shed by the side of Loch Tay. I briefly mentioned the area in chapter 6 in connection with steamer services on Loch Tay, but here I would like you to consider my Killin Junction and Killin branch scheme on the next two pages.

Above: McIntosh's 0-4-4Ts worked over many Scottish branch lines after the grouping and lasted well into BR days. This 7mm model on St Catherine's for Loch Fyne was built from a Meteor kit.
(Photograph: the author)

Right: a Holmes J36 No. 65313 on Loch Lochy (plan below) operating in steam mode. *(Photograph: Steve Flint)*

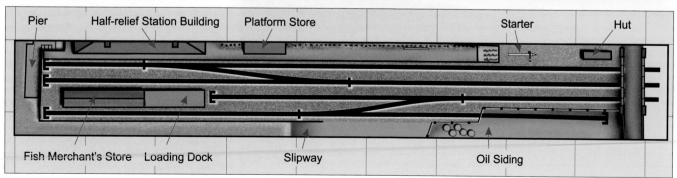

Pier — Half-relief Station Building — Platform Store — Starter — Hut

Fish Merchant's Store — Loading Dock — Slipway — Oil Siding

KILLIN TO KILLIN JUNCTION

Killin Junction was one of those remarkable railway stations serving a picturesque branch line which, somehow, managed to remain steam operated until its premature closure in September 1965. The branch ran from Killin Junction down the valley to the diminutive Killin station, serving the village, and its eventual terminus at Loch Tay. The gradients were tough and outward from Killin there was ferocious climb back up to the junction. Passenger services on the branch rarely required more than one coach. The most common form of motive power used on the branch, was in the shape of the delightful ex-Caledonian Railway 0-4-4T Class 439, although towards the end of the operations, a BR Standard Class 4 tank engine performed the duty, usually with an ex-LNER Thompson steel sided non-corridor brake third coach (below). As mentioned in the main text, the branch and the main line through Killin Junction were closed abruptly in 1965 because of a rather punitive landslip near Glenoglehead. Consequently, all services from Stirling to Oban via Callander ceased immediately, and were re-routed from Glasgow via the spur at Crianlarich. With the build up of tourism since that period, what a great shame it is that trains cannot run into the Trossachs region. Hindsight is a wonderful thing!

Killin Junction itself was a station without any noticeable access road and was quite a long but narrow site, very suitable for modelling. As well as the

branch activities, there were main trains between Glasgow, Stirling and Oban. Whilst this route was a longish branch line in its own right, well-proportioned passenger trains were hauled over the years by what should be considered as 'main-line' motive power. Many of the newest Caledonian Rly locomotives were found on the line in pre-grouping days and they continued in service during the LMS and BR periods. Diesels, in the main, were left to some of the early Type 2 examples including the Class 21s as well as the BRCW Type 2 Class 27s. Some DMU sets operated the Six-Lochs Land Cruise rail tours which ran down to Loch Tay on occasions during the 1950s and early 1960s.

The junction underwent a number of changes over the years, and there were for many years, two signal boxes at the station. The west box was closed after the 1935 alterations and the tall east box received additional levers. To model the line in late LMS days and through to closure will require nine turnouts, and of course it may be necessary to shorten the whole track plan a little in order to fit the layout into a reasonable space. Just outside the footprint of the station itself were some railway staff cottages, whilst facilities on the platforms were rather basic. There were two platforms: on the northern side an island platform with a wooden building located centrally, on the southern side was a single platform, again with a wooden building. The

Killin branch train used the northern-most platform (down platform), and utilised the loops in order to run round. A wooden footbridge linked the island platform with the other platform (up platform).

The surviving signal cabin stood between the main line and the branch and was a tall brick built affair. I think the branch dropped away from the junction at a steep 1 in 50 gradient whilst the main line began to climb eastwards too, creating a very noticeable height difference between them, as indeed I have seen in photographs. Perhaps the gradients could be incorporated carefully into a possible layout. At the opposite end of the layout, there were a couple of short sidings, no doubt used to store vans and wagons for the branch. The branch service operated frequently as a mixed passenger and goods train: one coach and a couple of freight vehicles was often the norm.

The plan is presented as a full room project, possibly a garage or loft, though each station could easily be modelled separately. It could be built and operated by one person, but due to its size might be more suited as a club or group layout.

The area surrounding the site of Killin Junction is not the highest of mountainous landscape, but the backdrop behind Killin is quite stunning. There are many beautiful photographs showing the Killin branch train crossing the River Dochart nearby to Killin itself: a spot which would make a super diorama. Scenically, treatment would be a combination of heather clad moorland with tumbling hillside streams interspersed with trees and shrubbery.

As mentioned on page 70 in chapter 6, the Killin branch could have been part of a much greater scheme. It had been planned to extend the Aberfeldy Branch to the northern shores of Loch Tay, with a steamer service sailing between the two.

Standard 4MT 2-6-4T No. 80093 is seen on the Killin branch in Summer 1965. Whether you model Killin, or a might-have-been branch, the new 4MT model from Bachmann fits the bill nicely.

(Photograph: Geo. N. Turnbull)

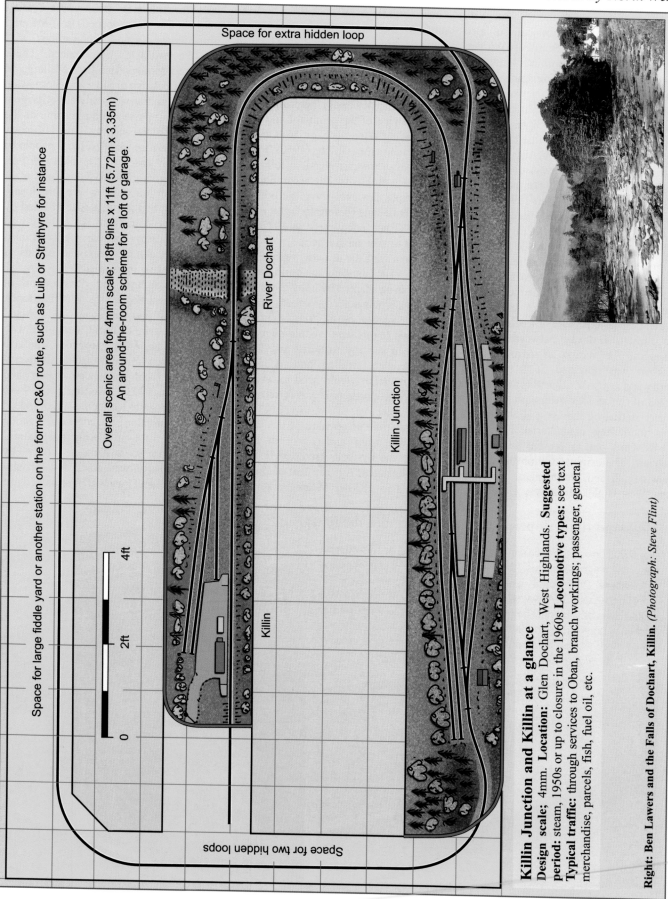

Space for extra hidden loop

Space for large fiddle yard or another station on the former C&O route, such as Luib or Strathyre for instance

Overall scenic area for 4mm scale: 18ft 9ins x 11ft (5.72m x 3.35m)
An around-the-room scheme for a loft or garage.

River Dochart

Killin Junction

Killin

Space for two hidden loops

4ft

2ft

0

Killin Junction and Killin at a glance

Design scale; 4mm. **Location:** Glen Dochart, West Highlands. **Suggested period:** steam, 1950s or up to closure in the 1960s **Locomotive types;** see text **Typical traffic:** through services to Oban, branch workings; passenger, general merchandise, parcels, fish, fuel oil, etc.

Right: Ben Lawers and the Falls of Dochart, Killin. (*Photograph: Steve Flint*)

However, returning to the original West Highland Railway proposal, it also included an extension from Fort William westwards through Glenfinnan to the tiny settlement of Roshven on the southern shore of Loch Ailort. This would have given the railway access to shipping serving the Small Isles and Skye. The line from Glasgow to Fort William received its Act of Parliament but the proposed extension to Roshven was quashed by local landowners and did not materialise. The route finally opened in 1894 becoming, of course, the original West Highland Railway, running from Craigendoran Junction on the north bank of the River Clyde, through Garelochead, and then by Glen Douglas to reach Arrochar at the head of Loch Long. The line then continued along the narrow neck of land to reach the western shore of Loch Lomond at Tarbert. Halfway between the two villages, the station of Arrochar and Tarbert was provided. It is still open today and is also a railhead for the movement of timber logs. Although just about every station on the West Highland line has modelling characteristics, I have chosen this one to present as a layout scheme. The original station building is now demolished, but the plan shows it in situ. West Highland Railway chalet style station buildings must surely represent some of the most characteristic island platform structures in the UK. Many of the stations on the line had a version of this eminently attractive design and thus it would be remiss of me should I not include one in this book: therefore a 2mm scale drawing of the original building at Ardlui is included on page 86. Original because sometime in the 1950s it was rebuilt as a shorter version following subsidence problems. The accompanying photographs however show the building in its rebuilt state (before in fact it had to be demolished completely in 1972 as a result of further subsidence).

So in a way, the drawing represents a generic WHR island station building, one which can be adapted by individuals to fit their own circumstances, perhaps built as a shorter version by omitting sections if necessary. In this vein it could be readily adapted to suit my Arrochar and Tarbet plan, though a fastidious and uncompromising modeller would need to research the exact proportions if a precise model was the objective.

At the time of opening of the WHR, plans were well under way to reach Mallaig: the by-then, preferred destination to Roshven. A great deal of finance was used in making Mallaig a suitable port for the rich west coast fishing market. The line opened in 1901 and immediately steamer connections with the Western Isles commenced. There were now sailings from both Mallaig and Kyle of Lochalsh to Skye and Stornaway.

That the railway between Glasgow and Mallaig passes through some of the most spectacular scenery in the UK is not disputed. It also assisted local people to travel with ease, to the likes of Fort William and indeed Glasgow, at a fraction of the cost, where previously people had had to use a coach hauled by horses. The coming of the railway also employed many people whilst it also enabled inhabitants from the islands to reach Glasgow more easily.

The planning and construction of railways continued in the West Highlands, much as it did far away in Highland territory as well. The Caledonian with their through, albeit circuitous, route to Oban, built a line to Ballachulish diverging off the Oban line at Connel Ferry and opening in 1903. This line could have been extended to Kinlochleven, or indeed Fort William along the coast and creating another might-have-been postulation: Fort William South perhaps, serviced by Caledonian Railway stock and locomotives. In the end however, it remained just

Highland timber operations - prototype and model

Timber is one of those commodities that can easily be transhipped onto rail wagons and just about any layout set in rural Scotland after about 1983 could justify a siding for this sort of traffic. Cambrian Kits' OTA wagons are seen on Paul Timperley's EM gauge Dalmally layout (below). Full size loading is witnessed at Arrochar and Tarbet in 2005 (right). It may only be a matter of time before we can buy a digitally controlled model grab crane!
(Prototype photographs, left and opposite: the author)

ARROCHAR AND TARBET

The removal of felled timber by rail has been a traffic source for many decades in Scotland and the relatively simple loading facilities make this an easily modelled topic.

In the main text I mentioned Kinbrace on the Far North line where a temporary loading area was provided next to the main running line. The train was halted alongside whilst a hydraulic grab loaded the wagons at night after passenger services had ceased.

However for modelling timber traffic operations I would suggest this station on the West Highland line. Here the original track plan in the goods yard has been transformed into a timber loading area (right). A lorry, with its own integral grab style crane loads the logs into special wagons (lower left). TOPS coded as OTA wagons, most of them were converted from earlier VDA vans or OBA and OCA opens.

The station at Arrochar and Tarbet is quite a narrow site, making it ideal for a small modelling project. It would make sense to include the platforms and station buildings, as any timber train loco invariably has to run round its consist, making the passing loops at Arrochar imperative. Scenically, the site is quite well populated with trees of its own and there are two railway properties, now privately owned at the entrance to the station. The station is reached from the main road by two steep access roads. The trackbed at Arrochar, like many parts of the West Highland, follows the contours of the terrain and sits on a shelf cut into the landscape. There is a road bridge just down from the station, and I have retained it on the model.

I've suggested a contemporary period for this scheme, so timber trains will undoubtedly be in the hands of that small group of RETB fitted Motherwell based Class 66s. Day-to-day passenger workings, at times made up of 6-car Class 156 DMUs, could be represented, with just a single 2-car unit on grounds of space and expense. Backdating to the mid 1980s is feasible too, enabling the use of Class 37s on loco hauled passenger trains and some additional through freight from the Fort William area. Earlier still and 'Timber P' wagons (converted from BR Standard plate wagons) were used for timber traffic when Class 27s reigned on the route.

Whilst principally designed for 4mm scale, it is eminently suitable 2mm, N gauge, but rather a large project for 7mm. Kits of OTA vehicles are available in 4mm in the Cambrian range and a 7mm scale kit is available too. For N gauge, I suggest the simplicity of the bodywork would allow conversion of 20ft 9ins wheelbase wagons in the Farish range. You can at least purchase ready made cast 'log piles' which are most suitable, but, a quick trip down a rustic lane will soon provide you with ample 'timber' for your loads and considerably cheaper too!

Arrochar and Tarbet at a glance

Design scale; 4mm. **Location:** West Highland line. **Suggested period:** it is envisaged as present day, but could be backdated. **Locomotive types:** Class 66 and 156 DMUs. **Typical traffic:** timber logs, Alumina, Scotrail passenger services, Fort William sleeper and special excursions.

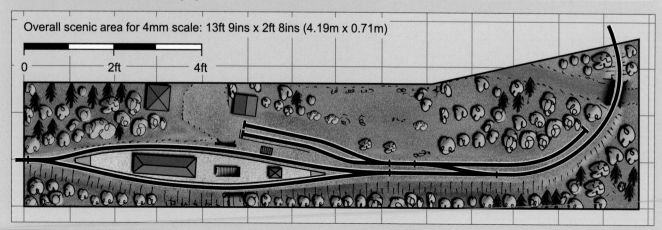

Overall scenic area for 4mm scale: 13ft 9ins x 2ft 8ins (4.19m x 0.71m)

0   2ft   4ft

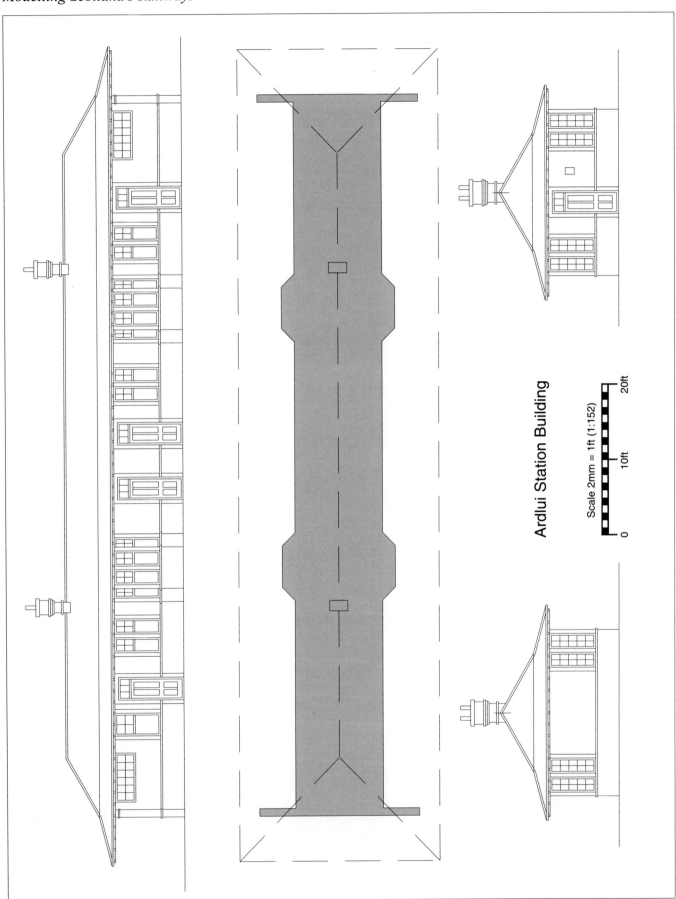

Ardlui Station Building

Scale 2mm = 1ft (1:152)

0   10ft   20ft

Ardlui, West Highland Railway

These are archive photographs now as the main building was demolished in the early 1970s due to subsidence. It had originally been a longer, standard length structure until cut back in 1955, I believe. A similar sized building existed at Craigendoran, the first station on the West Highland line. The drawing of Ardlui (left) however, shows the original version as built, thus anyone interested in modelling a typical West Highland chalet style building can use it as general guide. The platform signal cabin was also a standard structure, roughly eleven feet square. Many of the original buildings and signal cabins still exist on the line, it is therefore possible to measure them up if a dimensionally accurate model is required. *(Photographs: the author)*

a branch off the Oban line, closing in the 1960s but not before it had been dieselised with Class 27s working the old non-corridor stock. The Fort William smelter is well-known, but the smaller one at Kinlochleven also provided rail traffic to Ballachulish yard. The beautiful cantilevered design bridge at Connel, across the mouth of Loch Etive, which once accommodated both road and trail traffic, still stands today.

Other lines in the West Highlands include a distinctly local affair, which caused much bother at the time. A line between Spean Bridge and Fort Augustus was planned passing Invergarry as it went up the Great Glen. The Highland Railway were furious, whilst the North British had financial commitments elsewhere. It ended by the Caledonian Canal, but the intention was to reach northwards and Inverness. Sadly this was not to be and after a short period of the Highland operating the line, the North British took over and they settled down to operating the services until the passen-

ger trains were withdrawn in 1933. Freight continued and during World War 2, the line was fairly busy. It closed in 1946, but had it reached up the Great Glen, there probably would have been a station at Drumnadrochit. That of course takes us full circle back to chapter 2 and the Glasgow and North Western Railway proposal: what a super station name that would make for a model railway!

Below: a freight train composed entirely of parcels vans prepares to depart Loch Lochy. *(Photograph: Steve Flint)*

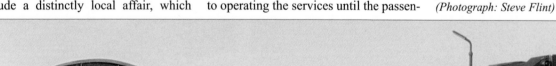

When the West Highland Railway opened, there was a small branch to Banavie, close to the Caledonian Canal. Eventually the Mallaig line continued westwards but a few services from Fort William to Banavie Pier station operated. The branch closed to passengers at the outset of World War 2 in 1939 and they were never reinstated although some freight lingered on. The histories of these railway lines have been recorded in many books and articles over the years. They were quite distinctive and typified life in the Highlands of Scotland. Despite the great length of some of the routes, they remained very much as local lines. Apart from during the years of the two great conflicts, and during the summer holiday periods, traffic could be sparse. Some modellers complain about the lack of variety with the motive power used on the lines, saying it can restrict the operating possibilities. Personally though, I feel this should encourage modellers to only purchase examples of such stock as they actually need, detailing the items to the best of their ability, and then operating them in prototypical manner.

That policy has certainly stopped me from dashing out and purchasing the latest goodie the trade has to offer - even if I had no immediate use for it. Such an attitude to new purchases should focus your mind to modelling actual locations or might-have-been localities, and therefore hopefully creating that special 'atmosphere' in the model that we all are pursuing.

Before leaving this chapter for North East Scotland, I present one final layout proposal that I think is suitable for most periods. The Laggan valley, recently immortalised in the BBC drama 'Monarch of the Glen', is ideally situated for linking the old WHR at Tulloch with the old HR main line at Newtonmore: a prospective route that has been postulated for decades, even in current times under privatisation, and one which a glimpse of even the most rudimentary road atlas will reveal itself.

So please pause for a short while at Kinlochlaggan, before recommencing your journey into Malt Whisky territory.

The Glen Douglas passing loop

During the dire days of the 1960s and 1970s, many of these passing loops in Scotland were taken out of action. A few have since been reinstated, because the operating authorities have actually found they cannot run services without them!

A loop still exists at Glen Douglas today, but so do some additional sidings and miles of high security fencing serving the MOD, making it an untidy scene. All that was in the future when I paid the site a visit and was able to photograph the signal cabin and its cottage without being chased by an Alsatian guard dog and an equally burly security guard!

I present these buildings as prototypes for use on the Kinlochlaggan scheme. *(Photographs: the author)*

KINLOCHLAGGAN

Loch Laggan, whilst not quite isolated, is situated in a mountainous region of the Central Highlands. The beautifully rugged landscape is completely dominated by the Bens and Munros which are found in whatever direction you tend to gaze in; Carn Liath, Creag Meagaidh and Beinn A' Chaorunn on its northern shore and Binnein Shuas overlooking its southern shore. Loch Laggan itself flows westwards into the smaller Loch Spean, which in turn flows into the River Spean, if you are looking for a typical Highland landscape you need go no further.

The nearest rail-head in the west is Tulloch station on the West Highland line; to the east, Newtonmore station on the Highland Main Line is possibly the closest. The distance between Tulloch and Newtonmore is about 25 miles. Strange to say, the NBR used to have a sign on Tulloch station, which stated that Tulloch was the station for Kingussie, which is, in fact, the next station up from Newtonmore on the Highland line!

From time to time there have been numerous proposals to build a line along this route. Indeed the earliest one was in the 1860s, supported but not to be financed, by the Highland Railway. The plans were dusted down several times; during the 1930s and again during the 1960s and 70s. Though nothing ever came about, a superb 'just supposing' type of layout is conjured up: scenic grandeur with an almost alpine like backdrop. This is mountain country and I feel quite sure the gradients would necessitate double heading. In more recent times, pairs of Class 37s and the like. Latterly, the newer Class 66s would be able to haul the freight single-handed, though a little bit of modellers licence would not go amiss.

Let us assume that the line was constructed in the early days and it had a typical West Highland feel about it. Let us also assume the operating authorities did not feel that passenger traffic would have a great influence on the route, dictating that Kinlochlaggan, (as it is roughly half-way between Tulloch and Newtonmore) would have been a passing loop with a signal cabin and perhaps a short platform for use by railway staff.

Similar scenerios to this were found at Corrour, Glen Douglas and Gortan on the West Highland. Corrour is still in existence and the buildings survive to this day, however, to give a flavour of how this layout might look I have included (opposite) some views taken at Glen Douglas quite a few years ago.

From my delvings, it would appear the line would have been useful for Aluminium related traffic to and from the British Aluminium plant in Fort William. A further traffic along the line of course, would be timber. This traffic increased during the 1980s: an excellent period in which to set Kinlochlaggan as redundant VDA vans were being converted into OTAs. In a similar vein, finished paper products from Corpach could well be sent over the route in VGA vans and Cargowaggons. There is also talk of an integrated sawmill, pulp and paper mill and renewable energy regeneration plant for Invergordan in Easter Ross. Due in 2008, this would create modern day traffic sources for the layout.

Finally, although passenger services were not envisaged, they could be included, and why not consider the route for specials: a set of Pullman coaches or specially painted stock to represent one of those swish tourist style workings, like the Royal Scotsman, would bring a little colour to what is basically a freight only line. The Laggan cut-off, as I like to call it, would be a God-send to the operators of such services. All sorts of locomotive variations would become available, perhaps top and tailed: pairs of 37s or 47s as well as the FM Rail Class 31s. The SRPS would instigate trips via the line, perhaps hauled by a preserved Class 26 or 27, or better still the LNER K4 No. 3442 'The Great Marquess'. Quite a wide selection of stock for a small and rather lonely passing loop!

Kinlochlaggan at a glance

Design scale; 4mm, but adaptable for 2mm especially if set in modern times. **Location:** Central Highlands. **Suggested period:** contemporary diesel era but adaptable to any. **Locomotive types:** see text. **Typical traffic:** freight only; timber, fuel oil and aluminium related, special excursion passenger workings.

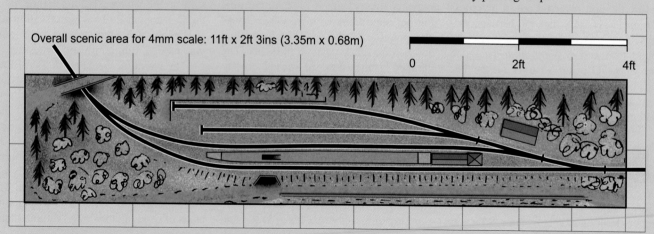

Overall scenic area for 4mm scale: 11ft x 2ft 3ins (3.35m x 0.68m)

0   2ft   4ft

Chapter 8

North East Scotland

This area of Scotland, between Inverness and Aberdeen, was a fairly unknown quantity to me until very recently. True, I had, at one point in deep and distant history, travelled between these two cities on one of the old Class 120 DMUs, leaving my camera bag on one of the front seats as I remember, but retrieving it before the unit reversed out of Inverness station to set back into the carriage sidings. That was in the days of black and white film and was my first excursion into Scotland using a Rover Ticket. The territory was not my main area of interest then, and it remained more or less in the background for many years.

When one builds a model railway it is always pleasant to receive invitations to exhibitions: more so if they are from shows in unfamiliar territory where you have never exhibited before. In many ways I think I gain the most pleasure from exhibiting at such venues. So it was a complete surprise to be asked to take

my 7mm 'Otterburn' layout all the way from Norfolk up to Elgin during Easter 2005. Further, the visit would be a perfect opportunity to become a little more familiar with the region, and perhaps obtain some photographs. As a bonus, the long journey enabled me to look closely at the Highland main line as the A9 road keeps company with it for many a mile. Further opportunities arose when it was also possible to visit an old friend I had not seen for many years in Pitlochry. The planned route was to travel up to Newcastle where I would pick up Steve Corrigall, my trusty travelling operator, and head through the Borders to Edinburgh. We would then cross the Firth of Forth, make for Stirling and call and see my friend at Pitlochry before motoring further up the A9. There was then to be a short stop at Aviemore, in order to view the Strathspey Railway, before climbing across the moors to Dava and into the coastal strip to finally reach

Above: 'Glenbarrie' is a pastiche of the GNoSR branch to Portsoy in BR days and was built by members of the Moray Model Railway Group. The locomotive is an ex-Caledonian Railway Pickersgill 4-4-0 No. 54485. *(Photograph: Steve Flint)*

Elgin. The return trip was to head eastwards to Aberdeen, then an overnight stop at Stonehaven before calling in at the Caledonian Railway preservation site at Brechin. After that, a long drive south via Dundee, Edinburgh and Tyneside.

The resulting weekend in North East Scotland was not only fruitful, it was also extremely enjoyable. A number of visitors to the Elgin show commented that they had read about my layouts but never expected to ever see one because of how far they live from the usual exhibition circuits. That was extremely gratifying, and more so, as in the short time that was available to me, I was able to pinpoint areas of research to which I returned later in the year.

Right: a delightful station yard scene in pre-grouping days at Ballater, the terminus of the Deeside line. A model of this station, with attendant Royal Trains, would make for an interesting and authentic historical treatise.(Photograph: publisher's collection.)

Today, all that appears to remain of the railways in North East Scotland is the main line between Inverness and Aberdeen, although the branch to Burghead still has some track in place. As you pass through the region you can see at a glance that the whole area was more or less devoted to farming and fishing. I believe many of the small branch lines, now long closed, were dubbed 'farmers railways' because they were constructed to serve the vast coastal plain across the area. Much of the land was taken over for the growing of wheat, oats and barley, but root crops were abundant too, potatoes in particular. Consequently, whilst passenger traffic might have been disappointing to the early promoters, and the majority of the branch lines were local concerns, the freight traffic, although seasonal, would have been quite heavy.

There is of course one other industry important to this region: whisky distilling. As any whisky connoisseur knows, whilst there are distilleries in numerous other regions of Scotland, both island and mainland, the highest concentration of them lies within this part of Scotland. Despite the whims of the global market, the whisky industry in this region is still thriving and has in turn developed into a tourist attraction appropriately labelled the 'Whisky Trail'. You just have to stand near a distillery and the smells will get you swaying! As we shall see later in this chapter, railways played a key part in the whisky distilling business in the days before road transportation conquered all. Natural and raw ingredients were taken in by rail to the distilleries and the finished product was outshipped by rail to market also.

One of the earliest lines to be built in the region was that from Aberdeen to Ballater, opened in stages between 1853 and 1866, which of course was patronised by Queen Victoria herself, who had a residence at Balmoral further up the valley. The route followed the course of the River Dee and was relatively unchallenging in terms of significant gradients until the last few miles. Interestingly, the

terminus at Ballater was not the final intended destination and a road bridge was built over the headshunt end of the track formation. The hope was that the railway would run further up the valley to Crathie and Braemar, but possibly because Her Royal Highness was 'not amused' about the railway passing so close to her Scottish home, it never materialised. Nevertheless, here is another practical might-have-been extension that could be adopted by modellers, Braemar itself being a settlement on the edge of the dominant Grampian Mountains.

This branch saw trials of a prototype electric multiple unit in the late 1950s: the battery electric 2 car 'BEMU' based on the Derby Lightweight DMU bodyshell, and so can be modelled in 4mm by adapting a DC Kits kit. The 'BEMU' has had a chequered history: used by BR for testing purposes and christened 'Gemini', it was purchased by the now defunct West Yorkshire Transport Musuem and refurbished by the East Lancashire Railway. However, it is now happily back home, in the stocklist of the preservation group on this old line, the Royal Deeside Railway, which is based at Banchory Station site.

Because of its royal connections, the branch witnessed the passage of various Royal Trains down the years, although photographic evidence is somewhat scant. However, along with the battery unit, this provides for a layout scheme that would include some fairly unusual prototype stock. Before closure in the 1960s conventional DMUs, of Cravens

and Metro-Cammell types, were also used on the line.

Slightly to the north the inland town of Alford was reached by a line which also ran through undemanding countryside. It was opened in 1859, closed in 1965, but happily the site survives to this day operated by the Alford Valley Railway as a 2ft gauge tourist line. Perhaps not ideal for the purist modeller, but certainly a great day out.

As I mentioned earlier, the area between Aberdeen to the Moray Firth is a rich agricultural land with numerous fishing ports dotted along the coast. During the mid-nineteenth century, the area saw the emergence of quite long rural lines that trailed and meandered northwards towards the coast from what effectively became the GNoSR 'main line' route between Aberdeen and Inverness. This was achieved as the GNoSR eventually amalgamated the majority of the lines in the east of the region whilst they steadily built the main route through to Inverness. In the event, they got no further than Keith, where the Highland Railway had arrived via their line from Elgin. There was much animosity between the two companies, and if common sense had not prevailed, much duplication of routes could have occurred in the whole of the area. Although in some respects that could have been a bonus for modellers, providing lots of other prototypes to consider. In any case, modeller's licence allows us to build them anyway!

As usual, the local landowners wanted these lines built, although they frequently spent their time dipping their hands into the railways' pockets. So much so that they often lurched into financial crisis, though there is little doubt the lines served their communities well for many years. Most did not close until the mid 1960s, although a few lost their passenger services earlier and some lingered on as freight only routes until the late 1970s.

Within east Aberdeenshire, the bigger towns were those on the coast with buoyant fishing fleets and harbours. The main route served Peterhead and Fraserburgh, where a light railway was constructed from there to St Combs, and split at Maud Junction. At Peterhead a prison was built which no doubt gave the railway some unwanted customers: the North British Railway built a prison van which I believe used to go there. Although passenger services finished in

1965, Fraserburgh provided some railborne freight until final closure in 1979, and it is believed this included fish until at least 1973.

Another junction on the line at Ellon had a branch that went to Cruden Bay and Boddam, although this line was an early casualty, with passenger services ending in 1932 and the freight finishing in 1948. This was rather a pity since the emerging North Sea oil and gas industry of the late 1960s and early 1970s made its base here. Had the line survived, it could have become the railhead for construction traffic inwards or oil and gas condensate outward: a great raison d'être for a heavy industrial scheme powered by the various Type 2 Sulzers. In the event Maud Junction became the railhead and gas pipes for the St Fergus terminal were brought here for onward despatch. Further west a short branch left the main

line at Inverurie and went to Old Meldrum. It too lost its passenger services early on, in 1931 but the freight lasted until 1966. Inverurie itself became the main workshops for the Great North of Scotland Railway. The works were opened in stages between 1901 and 1905 with every department being transferred there. As a result, Inverurie became an important railway town and the works themselves, after the grouping, repaired locomotives from other Scottish companies and beyond.

Even in the 1960s, the works retained some work on diesel locomotives including, unfortunately, scrapping!

The next junction was at Inveramsay where a very long branch ran up to Macduff via Turriff. This was potato growing country, and a station close to Macduff had the fine name of King Edward, after the potato of the same name. Macduff was a fishing port and the station was a typical branch terminus complete with an overall roof for passengers, a small goods yard, a locomotive shed and turntable. It was as if it had been laid out with modellers in mind and Dave Elbourne from the Leamington Spa Club constructed a very accurate 4mm layout of Macduff, exhibiting it in the 1980s. One aspect of special interest to me, being a NBR man, was that regular locomotives working the branch in the 1950s and 1960s were the ex-NBR Glen class locomotives, transferred to North East Scotland from Eastfield. Sadly passenger services ended in 1951 (prior even to Beeching), with closure to freight following in stages in the 1960s.

From Inveramsay the main route continued west through Insch and Huntly. When I saw Insch on my recent visit I

INSCH

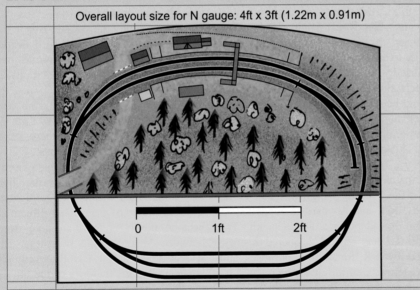

Overall layout size for N gauge: 4ft x 3ft (1.22m x 0.91m)

0   1ft   2ft

I have noticed at exhibitions that many N gauge modellers frequently fit quite an interesting scheme onto a single board, often only 4ft by 3ft. Insch is so designed to fit this handy space and could be a possible father and son (or daughter) layout located nicely in a small bedroom. Lifting barriers have replaced the original crossing gates,

but the signal cabin is still operational A small siding remains, probably for permanent way use and Scotrail liveried Class 158 DMUs operate the passenger services: one reason for suggesting this design in N gauge, as Bachmann currently offer a model along with the Class 66, which would be useful on through freight services.

Insch at a glance.

Design scale: 2mm, uses Peco code 80 track and curved and medium points.
Location: North East Scotland. **Period:** present day. **Locomotive types:** 158 DMUs, 66, 67. **Typical traffic:** contemporary freight and passenger.

Above: the station building at Insch, is representative of the structures along sections of the GNoSR main line and could be adapted for any similar layout project.
(photograph: the author)

was immediately struck by its modern day modelling potential. Again simplicity is the key and I have included it in the panel opposite as a possible scheme for N

gauge, perhaps for youngsters or new-comers to the hobby

So far virtually all the GNoSR route mileage was within the old county of

Aberdeenshire. After Cairnie Junction the GNoSR ran over the county border into Banffshire. The main route headed for Keith and the company's head on

BANFF

It was hard to choose between beautiful Banff or magnificent Macduff, the two delightful ex-Great North of Scotland terminus stations that faced each other across the Banff bay on Deveronside. Banff was the smaller of the two, so small it did not have platform run-round facilities. Opened as the Banff, Portsoy and Strathisla Railway in 1859, it ran a distance of six miles to Tillynaught Junction from where you could head south to the main Inverness to Aberdeen line, but the branch headed along the coast to Portsoy Cullen and Buckie and then eventually to Elgin. Originally the station had been named Banff Harbour, but the LNER changed it to Banff in 1928.

There was a neat wooden train shed at Banff with adjoining stone station buildings and, behind the passenger bay, were some incredible rocky out-crops which would make a splendid backdrop. There was a typical GNoSR wooden goods shed at the very end of the line. Behind all of these structures was an ancient gas works that would make an interesting model in itself. As seen on the plan there was a loading dock with a small crane and a further siding making an end loading dock, was quite a short spur. There was also a stone built engine shed and a small carriage shed. The turntable, for the small locomotives of the time, was taken out in the early 1900s: it was so small, the locomotives and tenders were uncoupled and turned separately! The whole site was separated from the

North Sea by a road and a slight embankment and was on a falling gra-dient such that trains were shunted back into the platforms by gravity.

Certainly a neat and compact sea-side terminus that could be made to fit on quite a narrow set of baseboards, although to do the scene justice, it would be interesting to at least include some of the sea shore as shown. Until some CR tank locomotives were drafted into the area, the graceful GNoSR D40 and D41 4-4-0 classes, and of course earlier types, operated the services. BR Standard 2MT 2-6-0s appeared regularly in the 1950s and

even the North British Class 21 diesels were reported on the branch.

Fish traffic would have been heavy at various times of the year and appropriately, some excellent kits are available in 4mm and 7mm. There would be incoming van traffic and general merchandise as well, with coal for domestic usage and also for the nearby gasworks no doubt.

Never a busy branch, it was the last remaining steam operated branch north of Aberdeen. Under the Beeching axe passenger traffic ceased on 4 July 1964 with freight lasting until 6 May 1968. *(Below: Banff in 1960. John Robin)*

Banff at a glance
Design scale: 4mm. **Location:** North East Coast. **Suggested period:** suitable for pre-grouping - 1960s to choice. **Locomotive types:** see text.
Typical traffic: passenger, fish, coal, agricultural produce etc.

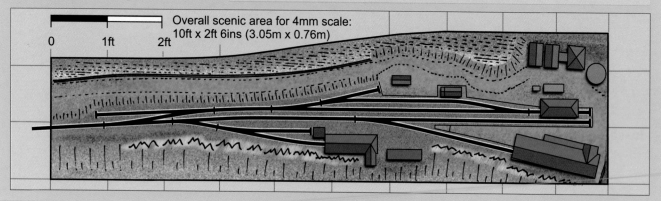

Overall scenic area for 4mm scale:
10ft x 2ft 6ins (3.05m x 0.76m)

0   1ft   2ft

confrontation with the Highland Railway, whilst a branch headed north eastwards through Glenbarry to Tillynaught. Here another fine country junction station was built which had incredibly beautiful glazed canopies and has recently been the subject of a 7mm model by members of the Aberdeen Model Railway Club. At Tillynaught Junction the route divided, with one branch going to the coastal port and county town of Banff, a most delightful station, and one which I have included as a layout scheme. The other route followed the coast itself to Portsoy, Cullen and Buckie, eventually linking back with the main HR route at Elgin. A short branch to the fishing port of Lossiemouth also linked Elgin. Because of the Highland's stranglehold, the GNoSR could not reach Elgin on a direct line but managed to end up there in a most roundabout fashion. As well as the circuitous coastal route, they also inherited a rambling line through to Elgin from the South. This was originally the Keith to Dufftown line which then headed north west to Elgin through Craigellachie

and Rothes. For many years after closure to passengers, the branch to Dufftown survived serving a grain railhead which lasted almost to the end of Speedlink services in 1991. It avoided the indignity of being lifted and has now been preserved. Today 1950s style DMUs operate the services from a refurbished Keith Town. It is hoped the preservation society can eventually use the attractive station at Keith itself, as the tracks are still connected to the main route between Aberdeen and Inverness.

The original station building at Dufftown (see page 25) has recently been refurbished into its original condition. It is of a standardised design used extensively over the western area of the GNoSR, constructed either of stone or timber, and could, once measured up, be scratchbuilt for a typical GNoSR layout.

Dufftown brings us to what is perhaps the most attractive part of this region. Although it is hard to choose between this, the Deeside area and the coastal branches, I would settle for the line serving Strathspey which ran from

Criagellachie Junction up the valley to Boat of Garten.

Here also the Highland Railway was to be found, with their line from Aviemore to Boat of Garten and then across the vast moor of Dava to Forres on the Inverness to Aberdeen line. This was their original main line south until the newer route via Culloden, Moy and Carrbridge opened. The Strathspey branch of the GNoSR was the company's own 'withered arm' that stretched to the very western end of their territory at Boat of Garten and it ran right through the middle of the whisky producing region.

Today, although devoid of railway, parts of the old route remain in use as a public bridleway, so one can still wander along the old trackbed and absorb the spirit of the old line. Several station buildings and other structures remain too, so go armed with a tape measure for essential research. The extra appeal of this route has to be the close proximity to the railway of several whisky distilleries, most of which were connected to the line in its heyday. Adding a lineside industry

Another scene on 'Glenbarrie' with 'Dailuaine', the Andew Barcley 0-4-0 saddletank. The prototype was used on the Dailuaine Distillery's private tracks which ran for about a mile from the junction with the main line. A similar set up existed at Cromdale for access to the Balmenach Distillery. *(Photograph: Steve Flint)*

to a layout is nothing new of course, but distilleries, with their characteristic malt kilns and bonded warehouses, must surely be the most attractive 'industrial' structures anyone could want as an adjunct providing extra sources of traffic, as indeed the watercolour illustrates.

An added bonus for modellers was the fact that some companies employed steam shunting locomotives working within the confines of the distillery in order to move rolling stock around. In some instances these worked into nearby stations or yards and so they could sometimes be seen next to main line locomotives, including some of the early diesels. One well photographed example of the distillery owned locomotives was the 0-4-0 Andrew Barclay belonging to the Dailuaine distillery, a model of which is shown on 'Glenbarrie' (left).

Even without the distilleries the Strathspey line was beautiful and I have included below some details of 'Blacksboat', one of the smaller stations along the route, and one that would make an excellent small layout project, particularly if tackled as a finer scale project in any of the scales.

Blacksboat

Named after a ferry that operated across the River Spey close by, this delightful little station still has the platform and buildings intact nearly 40 years after closure. The ferry was replaced by a bridge in 1911 and the station was enlarged to include the two sidings shown on the plan below which was prepared from an old photograph.

Above: when photographed in 1995 the goods shed was still in good repair, albeit in use as a hay barn! The station is still accessible via the Speyside Way and thus can be easily measured up for modelling purposes. *(Photographs: Steve Flint)*

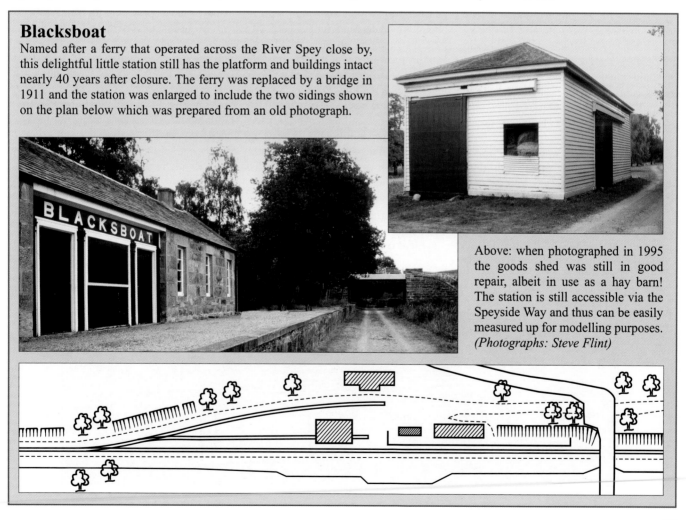

CARRON

The Spey Valley is a very attractive part of this region, noted for its scenery, salmon fishing and, of course, the finest *liquid gold* - malt whisky.

The Highland Railway reached Boat of Garten from Aviemore along the upper reaches of the valley, but then headed northwards across Dava moor in order to reach the north east coast. Meanwhile the Great North of Scotland Railway had opened their own line up the valley as far as Abernethy in 1863, extending it through to Boat of Garten in 1866. Much of this most delightful route clung to the banks of the river, twisting and turning through wooded enclaves and close beside the rushing white water that crashed and cascaded over the rocks. The river itself was, and still is, as significant as the landscape it passed through, for, as any connoisseur of whisky will tell you, the source of water used in distilling is vitally important.

As well as picturesque wayside stations, there were a number of whisky distilleries which were rail served right up until closure of the line. So you would have seen incoming grain, in particular barley as well as malt. Coal would have been required in some quantity whilst the finished goods would have been transported away in vans, or indeed in open wagons, the casks all neatly in place with their precious cargo safe inside. You did hear stories occasionally about whisky trains having accidents, and the resulting disappearance of the barrels or contents! Many of the distilleries had their own locomotives, frequently small 0-4-0 saddle tanks. They would be painted sometimes in bright colours and beautifully lined out, as well as invariably carrying the name of the owner's wife or whatever.

The Speyside line lost its passenger services in 1965, but freight throughout lingered on until 1968, with the final section, from Craigellachie to Aberlour, closing in 1971. Consequently, many of the freight trains were operated by the early diesels including the Class 26 - some in BR Blue - as well as in green livery. You could therefore have the sight of a 26, with open wagons full of casks, alongside a distillery Pug. Steam and diesel together, add the whisky, and what a combination!

Just over five miles west from Craigellachie was Carron. Here there was a simply magnificent stone and iron girder bridge over the River Spey: a scenic feature in its own right situated close to the simple passing station. That consisted of a loop and three sidings, one of which served a timber yard. Just passed the station on the opposite side was a turnout, which led into the Imperial Distillery. I have seen a photograph of the Andrew Barclay 0-4-0ST named 'Dailuaine' in Carron station: it must surely be heading for the Imperial Distillery. Apparently this little 'pug' had a plate attached to its cab-side stating it was allowed to operate on British Railways tracks. This probably meant it was allowed to collect wagons from the station itself, but may have inferred it could wander further afield?

Part of any distillery will be taken over with bonded warehousing where whisky is stored in a secure manner for many years in order to mature. Other features include mountains of casks stacked up in regimented rows and small clusters of outbuildings of considerable ages and construction. Also, usually tucked away in a corner, a small locomotive shed with perhaps basic servicing facilities.

This layout design, which has the largest scenic area of all the schemes in this book, follows the plan of Carron station and the Imperial Distillery quite closely. The only change I have made is to the size of the bonded warehouses, and although further compression is possible, I particularly like the expansive feel to this plan, something which I never have space enough for myself.

More practical perhaps would be to take a siding off your own branch line layout and fit a smaller system into the space you have available. Your emphasis may be on the internal shunting of the distillery, which would allow you to indulge in some quaint industrial locomotives, and if space allowed, some exchange sidings could give added operational potential.

Carron at a glance

Design scale: 4mm. **Location:** Speyside. **Suggested period:** 1950s - 1960s.
Locomotive types: ex-GNoSR steam, industrial steam, early diesels, railbuses.
Typical traffic: grain, whisky, coal, agricultural.

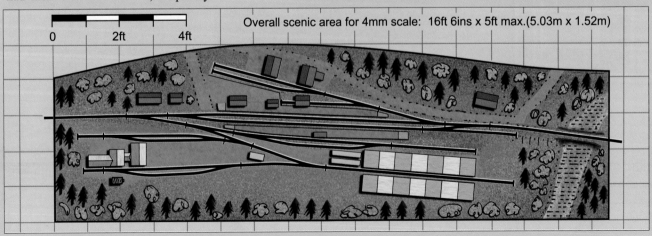

Overall scenic area for 4mm scale: 16ft 6ins x 5ft max.(5.03m x 1.52m)

0   2ft   4ft

In contrast, I have not neglected the distillery theme and include opposite a scheme based on the station at Carron which features the adjacent Imperial Distillery. Some further details on the Speyside route are also included.

It should not go without a mention of course that a distillery can be added to almost any Scottish based layout, particularly those set in the Highlands: there were a few Lowland distilleries as well, but only a very few isolated ones further south in the Borders region.

That the Strathspey and associated lines lasted into the mid-1960s is probably little short of a miracle, but there can be no doubt the sight of a graceful GNoSR 4-4-0 gliding around the curved trackwork of the valley would have been a joy to behold. Today the Strathspey railway lives on in part, with the preserved section between Aviemore and Boat of Garten over the old HR route. Scotrail and the The Strathspey Railway preservation group have made an extremely good job of renovating the station at Aviemore, complete with Highland Railway style signage and platform furniture. Much of the stock operated on the preserved railway is typical of that used in the area when the lines were in normal operation and is well worth a visit.

Whilst looking at this part of Scotland, mention of some proposed railway routes which never came about may give some further inspiration for layout building. Deposits of iron ore in the Grampian region got early promoters excited and several schemes were put forward which traversed some of the most desolate valleys in the central highlands. Several early proposals aimed to link Perth via Braemar and Tomintoul with Ballindalloch in Glen Spey and onward to an eventual destination at Elgin. Later ones included a line from Cambus O'May on the Ballater branch to Forbestown in upper Strathdon, then over Lecht pass, again to Tomintoul, but this time westward to Nethy Bridge (see map above). I recall an 0 gauge layout on the exhibition circuit in recent times called 'Strathdon' and set in the 1980s.

To complete our visit to this region we must now leave the GNoSR and turn to the lines of its old foe in the region: the Highland Railway. Along the North East

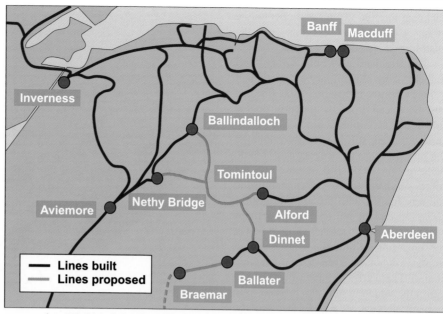

coast, the Highland built some small lines away from the main line. I have already mentioned the Burghead branch, which was the remaining part of the truncated Hopeman branch from Alves. Until the last decade, grain traffic was still using this route, certainly as far as the terminal at Roseisle near Coltfield and a recent exploration of the line revealed the trackwork still in place, though very recently, it has been cut back at Burghead as a result of a bridge removal. However, modern day modellers could, I am sure,

use their imagination, keep the branch open and have some very interesting workings with Class 66 and 67 locomotives. Of course a selection of Polybulk grain hoppers would be needed, which at the time of writing would require either conversion or scratchbuilding. Such vehicles must surely be in reasonable demand, and I find it difficult to understand why a major manufacturer has not produced one. The N gauge Society do have available, for members, kits of two Polybulk designs. You could naturally

Right: despite the decline of the traffic, a grain siding is still a popular adjunct to a post steam era layout. The terminal at Roseisle is one such prototype seen here with 37 410 on a rake of Polybulks in 1998.
(Photograph: Grahame Elgar)

Below: the N Gauge Society 'Grainflow' Polybulk kit.
(Photograph: N Gauge Society)

backdate the line further and operate the older CAO grain wagons or the Distillers-operated PAF wagons.

The Highland also built a very short branch to the old military establishment at Fort George. The route of this line can still be traced from its junction on the main line at Gollanfield. Some of the earthworks are still in existence although the line closed to passengers in 1943 and to freight in 1958. But assume that the route survived to make an interesting military branch with the opportunity for some unusual freight traffic and perhaps some Ministry of Defence motive power for operating within the confines of a military depot or even to the junction station. There are a number of wagon and van kits which could be pressed into military service to add further variety. Passenger traffic would be sparse, perhaps the usual single coach train with BCK vehicle running as a mixed train, or in the appropriate period, just a railbus.

Whilst not perhaps having the scenic grandeur of the more typical Highland setting, the lines of North East Scotland have much character. Apart from the main route between Inverness and Aberdeen, which is covered in more detail in the next chapter, the branch lines are totally suited to modellers who possibly prefer steam-operated layouts. However, several lines did survive long enough for the early diesels of the 1955 Modernisation Plan to run the services, in particular, it was possible to see green liveried EE Class 20s, NBL Class 21s and the Classes 24s and 26s. As well as passenger operation, there would be an interesting variety of freight workings, including fish, distillery or agricultural traffic, each with their specific van types.

Above: Another rail served distillery was the Knockdhu at Knock on the Buckie coastal route. NBL Class 21 D6150 is seen passing through with a freight in 1965.

Centre: Although devoid of its canopies in this shot, the grandeur of Tillynaught Junction is evident here as another NBL Class 21 D6153 arrives, also in 1965.
(Photographs: Roy M. Crombie)

Right: When photographed in 1994 the old station at Knockando on the Speyside route was 'preserved' as a whisky visitor centre.
(Photograph: Steve Flint)

Chapter 9
Along Main Lines

Left: the Scottish main line scene at the time of writing. A Glasgow bound Class 390 Virgin Trains 'Pendolino' sweeps through Carstairs in June 2006. Some ideas on layout configurations for main lines like the WCML are described in the main text.
(Photograph: Steve Flint)

Although many of the various main lines have been mentioned in the preceding text, it was felt that the major 'main line' routes were important enough to justify a section to themselves: particularly as a significant number of Scottish main lines remain in use today for both passenger and freight workings. It also needs to be noted that amongst railway modellers, branch terminus or the small shunting yard layouts are not to everyone's taste. There are many who enjoy the challenge, or perhaps yearn for an opportunity to model a stretch of main line, complete with large express locomotives and long trains of carriages or freight stock. I think the Scottish main lines fall into this category and though few of us have the space at home to recreate such dreams, it is often possible, if you are a member of a model railway club with spacious club-rooms, to get a group project going. Sometimes though, getting modellers to all agree on one location in a particular time-span, with the correct prototypical rolling stock can be difficult, although it is not impossible.

Right: a flavour of the main line scene in 1898 where the railway passes through Edinburgh Princes Street Gardens, though the train, headed by a NBR 0-6-0 No 415, is most probably a local service.
(Photograph: Dr T. F. Budden)

We all have our preference for modelling particular periods with the appropriate rolling stock, and many of us work in more than one period and location, and even scale. I like to model the former North British Railway branches in Northumberland, which also might include some 'might have been' locations. I also enjoy forays into the West Highlands: my preferred time period is usually 1951 for the former, and 1953 for the latter. However, I also have quite an affinity for the 'blue period' diesels

which worked in the West Highlands, and now, a growing interest in the current scene on the line too. What is perhaps not so obvious is my interest in the Waverley Route between Edinburgh and Carlisle. In Chapter 3 I made a fleeting remark about my favourite A3, No 60041 'Salmon Trout'. I could never see myself constructing a Waverley Route layout in my current modelling scale of 7mm, but such a prospect in 4mm could be quite interesting, and more to the point, much of the rolling stock for the LNER and BR period is readily available as ready to run in 00 gauge.

Despite my interest in town stations like Hawick or Galashiels, shortage of space would probably preclude such projects based upon these locations for me. I might consider tackling a smaller passing station, a rural junction, or an isolated summit of which the Waverley route has several. In this vein I have chosen Steele Road station to present as a layout plan on the next two pages. It is one which can be squeezed onto fairly narrow boards if (continued on page 102)

STEELE ROAD

There are numerous routes into Scotland if you are travelling by car, but I suspect the least used is the route up through the North Tyne valley. Scenically, it is stunning, as you commence along agreeable wooded valleys during its early stages, stumble upon small settlements which look as though they have not changed in decades, then climb onto moorland until you find yourself in the midst of a huge forest, surrounded on all sides by sturdy conifers. All of a sudden, you come across a vast expanse of water, this is the man-made Kielder Water reservoir. Travel further up the valley and the forest gives way to even more desolate moorland inhabited by seemingly hundreds of sheep, who graze by the side of the now very narrow road without a second glance as you pass by. As you travel on, you cannot fail to notice cuttings and embankments as well as bridges and structures, which indicate the track of an old railway. This is the route of the 1862 Border Counties line, but we are heading deeper into the fells, past Saughtree Fell and Arnton Fell to find the small wayside station of Steele Road, on the glorious Waverley Route.

The Waverley route opened in 1862 and was a double track main line which traversed stunning scenery but con-tained many fierce inclines and few straight sections of track. The drivers and their iron steeds were constantly challenged as timings between the Border towns were kept very tight. Despite this, the local traffic on this route, gave the distinct impression that time was not of the main essence, and for many years, the same sturdy NBR locomotives operated local trains with a timeless regularity, though providing an important service to the small communities along the route.

Steele Road was just one of those such small settlements, in actual fact just a row of cottages amidst the fells. One can assume that the main purpose of the station was to serve the agricultural needs of the many farms once found in that area. To the south was the small town of Newcastleton whilst to the North was that great Border capital, Hawick. The latter station was more or less the operating centre for the route right up until closure of the line in 1968. Riccarton Junction, the next station to the north of Steele Road was always just that, an extremely remote junction linking the Waverley Route with the Border Counties line.

From a modelling point of view, Steele Road would make an excellent project, especially in 4mm scale. This is because the likes of Hornby and Bachmann are now providing 4mm modellers with the classes of steam locomotives which operated the many services over the route. Coaching stock is becoming much better with Gresley, Thompson and BR Mk1 coaching stock, whilst freight vehicles are increasing year on year. I would envisage this layout to have the station as the main feature with a ladder of storage sidings behind. This would enable a procession of trains to pass by in either direction yet still allow the local services to stop for awhile, as well as giving a modicum of shunting in the very small yard.

The yard itself is basically a loop off the main line protected by a catch point. This means the yard can be shunted from either the up or down directions. There was a concrete style loading bank which originally had a cattle pen at the southern end of it.

There were few structures of note at Steele Road. A plain single storey station building, which probably had station staff accommodation at its rear, was on the down platform. Set into a gentle embankment, close to the entrance points of the yard, was a small signal cabin also on the down side of the line. An oil store was close to the signal cabin whilst a small bothy or hut was situated near the cattle pen. At the entrance to the station yard was a weigh-house, which was rarely used in latter days. On the up platform was a small wooden shelter for passengers. The harsh winds that blow across the fells would have made that small

Steele Road at a glance
Design scale: 4mm **Location:** Scottish Borders. **Suggested period:** 1950s.
Locomotive types: ex-NBR/LNER classes, BR Standards, Black Fives. **Typical traffic:** through passenger and freight, local passenger and pick-up goods.

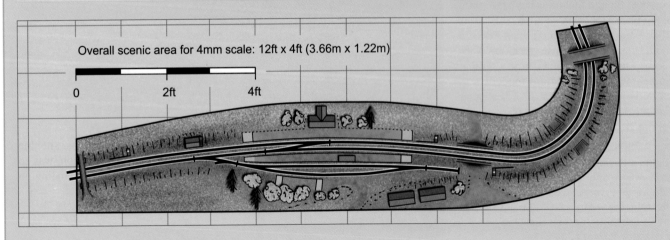

Overall scenic area for 4mm scale: 12ft x 4ft (3.66m x 1.22m)

0   2ft   4ft

Left: Steele Road station, seen during the 1930s. *(Photograph: Lens of Sutton)*

the Peebles loop (see page 36).

For historical accuracy, a little research would need to be carried out with reference to actual locomotive workings. Carlisle Canal had four A3s, which were more or less dedicated to working over the Waverley Route. Edinburgh St. Margarets shed and then Haymarket shed in the latter years had a similar arrangement with their Pacifics. A set of A4s allocated to St Margarets in the 1960s, operated the Millerhill to Kingmoor freights if a diesel was not available. However, the NBR designs, especially the 4-4-0s and 0-6-0s worked the line for many years and Scott class locomotives previously mentioned were allocated to Hawick throughout the 1950s until the mid-1960s. Towards the end, Hawick shed was served by BR Standard classes.

This design naturally fits into the 'main line' section of the book as it was a premier Scottish main route. Some say it should never have closed, being an excellent diversionary route should the East or West Coast routes be blocked. But close it did, back in 1969 despite vigorous opposition. However, plans are afoot to reopen the northern section of the route between Edinburgh and Galashiels, although some people would like to see it opened a few miles further on to St Boswells. There is also talk of opening the southern section from the WCML up to Riccarton and then down the Border Counties to Kielder so that the vast timber reserves can be transported out of the area. Trains might yet again pass through Steele Road, although a fair amount of trees would have to be taken from the station area itself, as it is now quite overgrown. Another good reason to model the line in the 1960s, would be the fact that very few trees will be required to be modelled, only those next to the station building.

On my last visit to this site the station, in its desolate isolation, was so beautifully silent, though standing in the old six-foot way on the bridge over the road, I swear that I heard the distant shriek of a Gresley whistle – magic!

structure very popular with waiting passengers. The cottages, which still remain to day, along with the main station buildings, were possibly railway properties, housing the platelayers who were employed to keep the permanent way in good trim.

Just slightly north of the station was an under-bridge, which took the line over the minor road which actually links the settlement with the main Newcastleton to Hawick road and the road which leads to the North Tyne valley. The bridge is still in place and, still heading towards Riccarton, the line curves away around the impressive Arnton Fell on a superb embankment. This would make an excellent entrance from any hidden sidings and would show off locomotives and rolling stock to the full. A couple of cattle or sheep under-bridges would not go amiss here. To the south, a gently sloping cutting is formed: here on the model a typical North British timber and rail built cattle-crossing bridge would make an excellent exit into the hidden sidings. As the line was still on the 1 in 75 ascent to Whitrope Tunnel, just north of Riccarton, locomotives passing northwards through Steele Road would be working quite hard.

In the period suggested, ten years or so before closure, traffic was actually at its greatest volume for many years, despite the local freight being rather run down. There was still a full service of passenger trains between Carlisle and Edinburgh as well as local stopping services from Edinburgh to Hawick and then Hawick to Carlisle. The NBR Scott and Glen classes from Hawick shed took these workings along with some of the more modern BR Standard classes as well as the D49s and K1s. However, an elderly NBR C15 from Hawick could sometimes be pressed into service too.

Ex-LNER Pacifics, such as A1s, A2s and A3s along with some A4s, which had been relieved of duties on the ECML by the Deltics, operated many of the passenger and freight turns. B1s and V2s assisted along with some smaller 0-6-0s such as J39s or older NBR 0-6-0s. Once Carlisle Canal shed closed in the early 1960s, London Midland Region locomotives started to appear from the newly opened Kingmoor depot. This brought Black Fives onto the line, mainly on freights.

If your preference is for green diesels, this could be just as interesting. Peaks took over many of the Anglo-Scottish expresses whilst the various Bo-Bo Type 2 locomotive classes took over local services. The sight of two Clayton Class 17s hauling long block trains over the line was, as it turned out to be, a risky business, as one of them would occasionally end up fire damaged! Towards the end of the line's existence, first generation DMUs operated some of the local services, not only on the Waverley route, but on other remaining branch lines, such as

Left: Bob and Gareth Rowlands built the railway through Princes Street Gardens in N gauge. An example of an uncomplicated continuous run layout with plenty of main line operating potential for the ready to run enthusiast. *(Photograph: Steve Flint)*

necessary, perhaps around the walls of a garage, cellar or loft room, or as a free-standing exhibition style layout. A copious fiddle yard would be required to accommodate lots of trains to recreate a busy day on the line. An example of this approach, though featuring a much wider scenic area (under which the fiddle yard is partly hidden) was built in 4mm, 00 gauge by Peter Kirmond from Leeds: though he chose Blea Moor on the Settle to Carlisle route in England. His layout consists of the main line with up and down goods loops, all set amongst the barren fells. Trains are simply allowed to pass through the scene creating an endless procession of workings, all with the correct rolling stock and locomotives for the period modelled. The Waverley prototypes, Whitrope or Fallahill, and the other main line routes throughout Scotland, provide inspiration and subject matter for the construction a similar style of layout: a configuration which would be ideal if you have an extensive collection of rolling stock and, of course, a large enough space in which to put it.

So, let us look at some of the other main lines starting with perhaps the oldest: the Edinburgh and Glasgow Railway which opened in 1842. It started as an independent company but was eventually taken over by the North British Railway, much to the disquiet of the Caledonian Railway it has to be said. The line between the two cities followed the Forth and Clyde and Union Canals, and apart from the steep incline out of Queen Street station, which caused many operational

difficulties until the arrival of the diesel age, the route was easily engineered and was intended as a high speed main line from the outset. The original promoters knew exactly what to expect in the way of financial returns from such an undertaking, as it was common knowledge that the nearby canal systems had made considerable profits from passengers and freight. The Edinburgh and Glasgow Railway eventually purchased the Union Canal in 1849.

The line set off from Glasgow and ran via Cowlairs Incline, Bishopbriggs, Kirkintilloch, Croy, Castlecary, Falkirk, Polmont, Linlithgow, Winchburgh, Ratho and Corstophine to Edinburgh Haymarket. It was extended in 1846 through the Princes Street Gardens to terminate at Waverley Bridge adjoining the North British station which had just opened, and from which services ran to Berwick upon Tweed. It is perhaps a testament to the original engineers that the line remains today, much as it was when it opened, with many of the stations mentioned above still open for business. During its lifetime it witnessed E&GR, NBR, LNER and British Railways operating a series of express services between the two cities especially as morning and evening commuter services, as well as a series of stopping trains which served the many stations on the route. Falkirk was always an important stop, being a junction for routes to the north, as well as an important centre for industry.

As a very early example of the 1950s move toward DMU operation, BR had

introduced the class 126 Inter City sets for the express services. By the 1970s, however, the developing road infrastructure between the two cities was having a detrimental effect on passenger receipts, so with much of the network seemingly in decline, British Rail decided to make the Edinburgh to Glasgow route a priority for increased traffic. In 1971 a push-pull mode of service was introduced with two Class 27 diesels at either end of a rake of six Mk2 coaches. The passenger workings were mostly half-hourly throughout the day, and success was immediate. By 1979 the intensive service pattern started taking its toll on the ageing Class 27s. They were replaced with a dedicated fleet of Class 47/7 locomotives and all of the locos were eventually named. The push-pull configuration was retained, this time with a 47 at one end and a specially designed Driving Van Trailer (converted from Mk2d BSOs) at the other end. The other coaches were of Mk3 pattern and so the sets were fully air conditioned. They continued the operation for many years, later including timetabled runs to Perth, Dundee and Aberdeen, and received the late 1980s Scotrail livery branding. Prior to privatisation they were finally replaced with the new generation of DMU, initially by 158s, but the route nowadays is operated by some of the latest units working in Scotland. There is a half hourly service at most times.

Because of the amount of urban building alongside the line for most of its length, it can hardly be said to be a rural line. There are stretches of open countryside and in places the old canal system can be observed, but industrial style buildings and housing estates abound. Within Edinburgh itself, an interesting modern station has been built to serve a technology park aptly named Edinburgh Park. It is surrounded by numerous high-tech modern commercial buildings and in direct contrast to historical modelling, this would be a challenging project to reproduce in 4mm scale. On the other hand, many of the older style station

Right: the new station at Edinburgh Park on the former North British main line to Falkirk and Glasgow. A challenging architectural modelling project, no doubt, but one suitable for a narrow layout site and modern traction enthusiasts.

(Photograph: Frazer Hay, courtesy International Design Patnership, Glasgow)

buildings are still in place and there are some superb bridges and viaducts along the line. Therefore, plenty of opportunities for a 'watching the trains go by' style of layout, and you can still go along and observe the line in operation today, despite there not being much variation in motive power and rolling stock.

It perhaps needs to be mentioned that other 'main lines' linked the two cities, although they did not offer too much in the way of competition, and the preferred route was, and still is, that of the original Edinburgh to Glasgow Railway. The Caledonian main line from Carlisle to Glasgow ran via Carstairs, and they built a spur that went off to Edinburgh. This enabled the CR to link the two cities, and although still a round-a-bout route to this day, it is now electrified and used by GNER services from London to reach Glasgow via Edinburgh. Eventually the Caledonian had a more direct route built via Mid-Calder Junction and during the pre-grouping period, over fifty trains a day operated between the two cities each day. In between these two routes, were the vast mineral workings, which were originally shared between the two rival concerns.

Carstairs and the nearby Law Junction was built in 4mm scale by members of the Nottingham (Bulwell) Model Railway Society and has been exhibited for many years. It is also now being built in N Gauge by the East Neuk Model Railway Club: a classic example of the need to be part of a club to get the best out of large projects.

The North British also constructed an additional route between the two cities. It left the main route at Ratho and went first to Bathgate. By 1862 it had reached Coatbridge and the through service eventually entered the centre of Glasgow at the small terminus known as College in 1871. This route abounded with sharp curves and steep gradients so was never a threat to the main NB route. Despite this, it passed through the centre of the NB

colliery lines and so passenger traffic as well as freight traffic was very well served. Only the route to Bathgate remains, which was the site of the Rootes car factory complex, and car carrying services left that area to travel south to England, often traversing the Waverley Route before it closed in 1969.

South from the Central Belt there were four main railways that crossed the Border from England into Scotland. We have already looked at the Waverley Route in some detail: the other three were the Glasgow & South Western Railway line between Carlisle, Dumfries, Kilmarnock, Barrhead and Glasgow St Enoch, the ex-Caledonian route (now the West Coast Main Line) from Carlisle, via Lockerbie, Beattock and Motherwell to Glasgow Central and the East Coast Main Line from Berwick upon Tweed via Dunbar to Edinburgh Waverley. All except the Waverley Route survive today, though, as described in the panel on Steele Road, there are proposals to reopen parts of the route, and indeed, the Scottish Parliament has recently passed the Waverley Railway (Scotland) Bill with the aim of seeing trains running again by 2011.

Both East and West Coast Main Lines are electrified and with the variety of passenger and freight traffic, there are plenty of opportunities for modern day modellers to represent such flows in the

more modern idiom. Much of the freight travels to and from Mossend Yard, to the south east of Glasgow, and much of it traverses the West Coast Main Line. Over on the East Coast line, a modicum of freight nowadays operates close to Edinburgh bringing coal to power stations and cement from Oxwellmains Works. Alumina trains to the aluminium smelter at Fort William also pass over the line from Blyth in Northumberland. This traffic flow has used the East Coast line for a considerable number of years. The West Coast Main Line was electrified throughout in 1974, whereas it wasn't until 1991 before the East Coast route was fully wired.

At the time of writing, in 4mm scale ready-to-run, there are several models available of contemporary prototypes, including earlier examples of main line electric locomotives now withdrawn as well as those classes still operating

Both main lines from their London points of departure have their most stunning scenic sections where they enter Scotland. The East Coast line skirts the high cliffs with splendid vistas out to sea. It also traverses some fine agricultural sections with a magnificent reddish soil much in evidence, as it heads inland slightly towards Grantshouse, before meeting the sea again at Cockburnspath en route to Dunbar. In days gone by, there were plenty of small passing stations on

Right: the East Coast Main Line amidst attractive scenery at Cockburnspath where a northbound GNER service is seen in June 2006. To increase operating potential, modern era modellers could add some freight sidings based, perhaps, on those at the nearby Oxwellmains or Torpoint sites.
(Photograph: Steve Flint)

the line which were all served by the railway and no doubt had a daily pick-up goods service. Some of these rural stations were junctions, such as Burnmouth, for the Eyemouth branch, Reston, a large junction station for the Duns branch to Melrose and, nearer to Edinburgh itself, Drem, which still remains the junction for the North Berwick branch today. The station at Longniddry used to serve the branch to the old county town of Haddington (see page 37). Thus modellers looking at earlier times have plenty of choice with crack passenger and fitted goods expresses or non-fitted style pick-up freights and branch trains together with a huge selection of steam prototypes to choose from.

The West Coast route, though devoid of any 'coast' in Scotland, commands magnificent scenery on the treacherous Beattock Bank and in lofty Upper Clyde Valley. It is a testing route which in the past, has caused many operational headaches to the railway authorities. For many years, even during the diesel period, banking locomotives were stabled at Beattock station in order to assist both freight and passenger trains up the incline. Prior to 1974, Class 50 locomotives operated the principal services in pairs to maintain timings over Beattock (and Shap in Northern England) whilst the line was electrified. It is only with the advent of electric traction that the line seems to have been tamed. Nevertheless, you cannot fail to be impressed even today, as the trains pass through dramatic scenery and frequently accompanied by stagger-

Left: not a main line at all, but who could resist this shot of Moffat, the terminus of the short branch off the Caledonain main line at Beattock. This is just the sort of branch line station that could be tagged onto a wall-hugging main line layout as mentioned in the main text. Another CR McIntosh 0-4-4T, No. 55232, is seen in 1954 - a ubiquitous Scottish branch line engine if ever there was one!
(Photograph: W. A. C. Smith)

ing weather. Soon after, the route becomes encompassed within the environs of the Greater Glasgow conurbation and seemingly runs for many miles through an urban environment, to finally enter Glasgow Central station.

There were one or two branch lines off this route including the link across the Solway Firth from Kirtlebridge to the Maryport and Carlisle line at Brayton, a political line if ever there was one. A short link between Lockerbie and Dumfries once existed and an even shorter enchanting branch line from Beattock,

to a perfectly agreeable terminus station at Moffat. It remained open until 1964 for freight, with passenger operation ceasing ten years earlier (below). Further up, and a branch ran westwards from Elvanfoot to Leadhills and Wanlockhead, whilst the branch from Symington made a head on connection at Peebles with the North British route, although it was rarely used.

Certainly then, these two routes offer interesting main line modelling possibilities, but how best to tackle it? One feature of the routes that is helpful is that because they run through difficult terrain,

they rarely occupy sprawling sites. The constraints of the surrounding hills mean that stations were built at sites that were long and thin, with sidings and goods yards paralleling the main lines tightly. Thus, narrow baseboards, such as those that would fit around a garage that also has to keep the car in, would suffice. Such layouts would be of the 'watching the trains go round' type, but operating potential could be increased if one of the various junctions mentioned were modelled, perhaps even extending the branch to its terminus built on high level boards above one half of the main layout. The other logical alternative is to choose N Gauge, where you get much more railway for your space, though the choice of appropriate stock is, at the time of writing, more limited. With the advent of DCC Digital Control, it has become much easier to wire up such large layouts with perhaps a lesser chance of electrical problems spoiling the operation. Of course, it would not be a cheap option, but the price of DCC equipment is likely to come down in price over the next few years, and some of the additional benefits of using these systems includes lighting and sound simulation, the latter which can be most impressive and light years away from the original Triang/Hornby tender chuff sounds of the sixties!

Not forgetting the fourth and final main line into Scotland: the Glasgow & South Western route. This also traversed some equally stunning scenery, but more in the way of the moorland variety. There were a few branches off the line at the southernmost end of the line, one branch leaving the line just north of Dumfries and heading towards to Moniaive. It had the quaint name of the Cairn Valley Light Railway and was opened in 1905. There was traffic from local quarries, mainly for road building, as well as coal, livestock, timber and general merchandise. The line closed to passengers in 1943 but the freight traffic remained and allowed the branch to hang on until 1949.

The main line continued northwards over moorland and lonely passing stations as it headed up the Nith Valley towards Kilmarnock. The area around Kilmarnock is quite industrial with coalmines and iron-works, as we saw in chapter 4. The line heads north west until Dalry is reached, where it then turns to

the north east in order to reach Paisley before crossing the River Clyde, and originally, entering the G&SWR terminus at Glasgow St. Enoch (see page 53). The route has never been electrified, much of the traffic today consisting of DMUs, but the line is useful as a diversionary route when the West Coast Main Line is blocked or has engineering works being carried out. Sadly most of the intermediate stations in the scenic Nithsdale section are closed, although Sanquhar was reopened in 1994 and a freight line to an opencast mine at New Cumnock has been re-established. Possibly researching the route for a historical layout would prove to offer the most interest in this case.

North of the two great cities and the Central Belt, main line routes extended up into the Highlands and eastwards towards Aberdeen. Today the East Coast Main Line ends up in Aberdeen, but in pre-Grouping days the route across the Firths of Forth and Tay on those magnificent bridges did not belong to just one company. Indeed the last 50 or so miles from Kinnaber Junction to Aberdeen belonged to the Caledonian. This was the extension of their main route through the Strathmore valley and was introduced in Chapter 6, mainly to highlight the numerous branches off it.

This route from Stanley Junction, just north of Perth, ran through Coupar Angus, Glamis, Forfar and Guthrie to Kinnaber Junction just north of Montrose. The North British route north ended at Kinnaber Junction, their services having to traverse Caledonian tracks to reach Aberdeen. Many are the stories about the Kinnaber signalman holding up the different expresses and deciding which one to allow the prestige of entering the section to the north, and therefore being the first to allow its passengers to disembark at Aberdeen station. North of Montrose the route continues on to Stonehaven, from where it follows the coastline closely in order to reach the Granite City itself.

The Strathmore route continued as a main line through the Grouping years and into British Railways days. However, it could not last and once the small branch lines in the area lost their passengers services, some as early as 1951 with the last going by 1955, only the main route

remained. For a short interlude, following an unfortunate attempt at using the NBL type 2 diesels, the route witnessed a swansong period for Gresley's A4 Pacific locomotives. In the early 1960s, these had been displaced by the Deltic diesel locomotives on the East Coast Main Line and they operated many of the 'three-hour' Glasgow to Aberdeen expresses over the route, together with some workings to Dundee. More reliable classes of diesel did share the work however and in 1966, would once again take over. Passenger traffic on the Strathmore route ceased more or less in 1967 and the Glasgow expresses were then re-routed via Dundee, Arbroath and Montrose.

The EE Class 40s, with some assistance from class 47s, were very common on those services throughout the 1970s, until the class 47/7s in push-pull formations took over. They too eventually ceased and today the only passenger locomotive hauled trains to use the route are the Caledonian Sleeper services, now in the hands of the Class 67s. The GNER service between London and Aberdeen remains an HST working, but other than that, the services are usually in the hands of Class 158 or Class 170 DMUs. Though the heyday of freight is long gone, there is still the possibility of seeing some freight if it is diverted from the Highland main line. Of course, in retrospect much of the whisky associated grain traffic would have used this route, but, with the present use of grain discharge facilities for ships in Burghead harbour, it is possible that it will never see the likes of grain transhipments again.

Whatever your chosen period, there are some interesting stretches to model especially where the railway meets the coast with numerous bridges and culverts taking rivers and streams under the railway and down to the sea. In the past there were several small passing stations complete, as usual, with the daily pick-up freight and even if a prototype station does not appeal directly, a might-have-been contrivance would work equally well. There was, and still is considerable agricultural development all along the coast to Aberdeen, and this would have contributed to the traffic patterns. In recent times of course, the oil industry created a great deal more freight on the line, with long trains of pipes heading northwards and other materials linked with the construction industry, concrete in particular. For modelling purposes, this traffic creates interesting traffic flows and allows us to use some of the more specialist vans and wagons in our trains. Like the G&SWR main line, I feel this route, and in particular the sections between Perth and Aberdeen have been greatly neglected by modellers.

We can now turn our attention to two further main line routes, one of which heads north from Perth to Inverness, the other is the route linking Inverness and Aberdeen which was featured in the previous chapter. The Highland Main Line, as it is known, commenced at Stanley Junction just to the north of Perth; nowadays, since Stanley is a junction no longer, everyone accepts Perth as its southernmost point. Perth station itself is still quite a huge affair with little rationalisation to the building and overall roof. During steam days and even in the early diesel period it was a hive of activity, and the modern DMU sets which nowadays use the station look extremely lost within it. Many of the sidings are still in place but are taken over by weeds and trees. Even the small yard to the left of the line as you head northwards out of station, is in a sorry state, home to redundant coal hopper wagons the last time I looked.

Before long though, the beauty of the route becomes apparent. The line passes through the wooded areas around Dunkeld and proceeds to climb higher into the hills and amongst the eventual mountains. The River Tay is constantly in view, although once past the now closed station of Ballinluig (the junction for the Aberfeldy Branch) the river becomes a tributary of the Tay, the River Tummel, as we climb into Glen Garry and head for Pitlochry. Here, by adopting the just supposing approach, we could imagine a line branching off the main and running due west along the shore of Loch Tummel, with little stations at Tummel Bridge and Dunalistair, en route to a diminutive branch terminus at Kinloch Rannoch in the shadow of Sheihallion. Back on the main route continuing north, the line passes through the Pass of Killiecrankie, a steep sided gorge and a place immortalised and romanticised in Scottish History. Soon Blair Atholl is reached, the stations and signal boxes on this line, still to this day, are pure Highland Railway. The boxes constructed out of wood whilst the station buildings are in stone, and extremely distinctive in their design. What the wooden signal boxes must have been be like in the middle of a hard Highland winter, I do not know.

The summit of the line is at the very remote spot of Dalnaspidal and there are long passing loops here. On the trip to Elgin with my 'Otterburn' layout, we drove along the A9, which more or less follows the railway. A three-car Class 170 and a two-car Class 158 coupled together were heading up the line to Inverness: it was absolutely superb following the progress of this train in beautiful sunshine and surrounded by magnificent highland scenery. Even the North British in me waned a little at the thought of capturing this scene in model form. Not long after the Elgin trip I purchased some suitable 4mm rolling stock, which is typical of the current scene up in the Highlands - rather worrying really: yes, it is actually, because I have since purchased some more! Not only that, I also recently travelled up to Inverness using the Sleeper service and that was quite an experience: or was it an adventure? Perhaps another story to tell some other time.

Once over the summit the line wends its way to Dalwhinnie and Newtonmore. This latter station could have become a junction station if a plan to build a line from Tulloch to Newtonmore had materialised (see page 89). That would have increased the Class 37 presence in the Highlands although I suppose a new line like that would have been engineered from the outset for larger locomotive types, and if it had been built, the Class 66 would be in charge of most of the workings now. Mind you, if a passenger service had been instigated, such a route could have meant people from Mallaig and Fort William could reach Inverness comfortably without having to resort to the A82 and the Great Glen. I have been told that if you live in the Lochaber district and have any other illness apart from perhaps, a sore finger, they airlift you by helicopter from Fort William hospital to Inverness! I am sure that is not really true, but why let the truth get in the way of a good story...

Kingussie station still remains open but soon the line reaches Aviemore, where you can join a steam train on the Strathspey Railway to Boat of Garten. The line drops a little in height towards Carr Bridge before a final assault up to Slochd summit. It then descends through Moy, whilst the view from the Culloden Viaduct is simply remarkable. Soon the line is approaching Inverness itself. The

Left: short, loco-hauled main line trains have always featured strongly in Scotland and this 1990 view of 47701 crossing Findhorn Viaduct on the Highland main line illustrates the point well. Majestic viaducts like this are perhaps most suited to N gauge though.
(Photograph: Steve Flint)

Left: today's railway scene is often much maligned for lack of variety, but this shot of modern Class 66 traction at Millburn Yard, Inverness in 2004 has a lot of tempting modelling appeal. After all, the locomotives are available ready-to-run in both 00 and N Gauges (*Photograph: Graeme Elgar*)

station has quite an unusual arrangement of platforms along two sides of what is effectively a triangular site, with the old Lochgorm shed situated in the apex. It seems to work extremely well, after all it has done for years, and I have often thought that Inverness station would make a good model layout if you had the correct amount of space. Thoughts of Black Fives about to depart to Kyle of Lochalsh or Wick and Thurso come to mind, standing out in the open along the platforms because of the very short train shed at the terminus end. I never saw the old steamers there myself, but I was about just early enough to photograph a few green and blue-liveried Class 26s, which had the first style of new numbers, pre-TOPS but without the 'D' prefix.

There are some lovely settings on the Highland Main Line, yet few modellers have attempted to capture the scene. John and Ian McReadie have accomplished it though, with their 20 year-plus project of Blair Atholl in the 1970s. Built in 4mm scale, 00 gauge it is a splendid historical biography of the locality and includes sections of the Tilt valley and parts of the village, all faithfully reproduced. One Highland layout that got away however, was Peter Tatlow's P4 'Killiecrankie' project, although he did tell me once that the boards are still about. I am sure it would have been a magnificent layout, especially if operated with those lovely mid-green liveried Highland Railway locomotives and rolling stock, or even the enchanting LMS period when the stock was in crimson.

As mentioned in chapter 8, the main line between Inverness and Aberdeen involved two pre-grouping companies; the Great North of Scotland Railway and the Highland Railway. The numerous branch lines which spread out from this line have been described earlier, but all that remains nowadays, apart from two small branches, is the main line itself. It is 108 miles long and, after leaving Inverness, follows the coast of the Moray Firth as far as Alves where the remnants of the Hopeman branch heads up to the coast to Roseisle and Burghead. From Elgin, the line heads inland, crossing rich agricultural land until Keith is reached, where the Keith and Dufftown Railway preservation group has taken over the branch with plans to use the branch platform at Keith station. Until recent times there was a rail served whisky bottling and distribution plant here and special purpose built bulk containers that ran on air-braked 4-wheel container flats, TOPS coded FBB, could be seen.

From Keith, the line heads further inland to Huntly and then through the lovely wayside station of Insch before reaching Inverurie. The next station of any importance is Dyce, right next to Aberdeen Airport. Nowadays a half hourly service into Aberdeen serves travellers and commuters alike and once upon a time it had been planned to extend this service southwards to Stonehaven. Aberdeen station is a large affair, still with much of its original pre-grouping architecture and has lots to interest modellers, though a faithful model would

surely be a large one. The station itself is today very bright and spacious with freight sidings immediately adjacent and the docks a little further away, but all within comfortable walking distance.

After the usual retraction of local and branch services along the line in the 1950s and 1960s, a scheme to improve the timings between the two cities was instigated. Class 120 DMUs were employed and took about two and a half hours for the service with about four intermediate stops. Occasionally the sets were strengthened with Class 122 single units and the pick-up freight traffic of the day was handled by the NBL Type 2s or later, the ubiquitous Sulzer-engined classes. The Beeching Plan had closed most of the smaller stations on the line and the track was singled, which in turn abolished many of the signal boxes and loops. From the 1980s, locomotive hauled trains took over from the ageing DMUs. Services were initially in the hands of Classes 26 and 27 with five coach rakes; later, class 47s were diagrammed, with maybe a 26 or 37 substituting if the class 47s were absent. They held sway until the arrival of 158s at the turn of the decade. The 158s are still in charge today, although the First Scotrail liveried class 170s are becoming more common. What freight there is today is in the hands of the usual class 66s and 67s, although sightings of class 37 and 47 are not unknown. Alas the variety of stock is not to be seen along the main line nowadays but the line has some pretty locations, and it is obvious the stations were extremely busy in days gone by.

Some time ago a container crane was installed at Elgin which still has a fair number of sidings. Over time it has received container flats, as much Government material arrives there for the nearby RAF station. Whilst on a recent visit there were huge numbers of coal hoppers standing idle on the tracks. Looking down from the road bridge, on one side you have a fairly typical modern booking office, sited on one of the two

Above: diverse freight traffic from private sidings survived on the GNoSR main line long after the end of traditional pick-ups. Here is one example with 47 289 on china clay slurry tanks seen leaving Inverurie for the Port Elphinstone depot in 1991.
(Photograph: Graeme Elgar)

platforms which are linked by a footbridge, although I fear it seems to be mainly used by the customers going to the ASDA store, which is right next to the station! To the north is a small signal box and on the other side of the road bridge, a further signal box, which possibly still looks after the small yard. This would actually make an interesting small shunting yard style of layout, using the road bridge as a scenic break. Container traffic would form the bulk of the freight services along with fuel oil and perhaps even some aviation fuel traffic. The passenger line curves away from the small freight yard, so could be easily placed along the front of the layout to its own dedicated siding in the fiddle yard.

A further 'just supposing' scheme could be a short line into RAF Kinloss, perhaps branching off at the former Kinloss station itself. It certainly would appear that military style layouts are becoming quite popular these days and can be justified by the diversity of traffic observed on such lines. Living close to USAF and RAF bases myself, I know times of conflict usually indicate greater patterns of traffic, so intense operation is not out of the question at such, albeit unfortunate, times. There is the added possibility of using industrial shunters too.

Once again, the Inverness to Aberdeen main line seems to be neglected by the modelling fraternity. By scratching the surface just slightly, quite a number of interesting modelling projects could be sourced, whether your interest be pre-grouping, the LMS and LNER period, steam operated British Railways or the post 1960s. Much of the infrastructure left in place gives you a clue to its origin, and that adds character to a layout even if it has been set during the present day. Nevertheless it is an ideal main line really, operating generally with both short passenger trains and short freight workings in whatever period you model. A lot of the motive power and stock used on these routes in the diesel era is available in 4mm scale, with a growing selection becoming available as kits in 7mm. For devotees of the micro-scales such as N Gauge, the modern scene is possible with Graham Farish producing the Class 158 DMU in Scotrail livery and the recently introduced Class 66. A comparatively expensive Class 67 can be obtained in this scale from a smaller manufacturer, but it is surely only a matter of time before a mass produced model will be made. Backdating to the steam era would however require a significant amount of kit building and scratchbuilding; that ought to be seen as a challenge rather than a shortcoming though.

That more or less concludes this section on main lines. Of course the definition of a main line is rather loose. I suppose there are some people who would argue that the Portpatrick and Wigtownshire line between Dumfries and Stranraer could also fit into the category of a main line: it certainly traversed some beautiful territory and had substantial freight traffic. More to the point, it was part of a route to Ireland and featured large express style locomotives like the Clan class. It is unfortunate that the line did not escape the pruning of the network in the 1960s, but as much of the route is still visible, perhaps more consideration should be given to it; in this connection, see my coverage in chapter 4.

In a similar vein, one of my favourite railways is the West Highland Line, and that was always described as a main line from the moment it opened in 1894. Just because a line is single track should not exclude it from being classed as a 'main line', though it does mean that passing loops become extremely important in the operation of such a route. In truth a high percentage of route miles in Scotland consist of single track sections, so Scottish main lines can either be double track, as you would perhaps expect, or equally, carry out their main line role with just a single track. That perhaps means that it can a little bit easier, as they require less space when modelled

Whatever the scenario though, Scotland's railways have been a source of modelling inspiration for me for most of my adult life. I hope that this book has demonstrated that, and whatever type of layout most appeals to you, I also hope that you too have become captivated by the awe, wonder, delight and immense variety that Scottish railways possess.

(i) Further Research

The Scottish Line Societies.

These five Societies based around the five pre-grouping companies are invaluable for information and archive material as well as supplies and resource information for modellers. Membership is open to anyone interested and each produce a Journal, usually on a quarterly basis, along with other specialised publications. Today, each Society is regarded as the definitive resource for research on the prototype and modellers seeking historical accuracy will find them invaluable.

As all positions are honorary, contact details may change from time, the details published here are correct at the time of writing. If in doubt a good starting point is the Internet, as all the Societies have a web site.

The Caledonian Railway Association
Chairman: Jim McIntosh, Secretary: David Coddington.
Membership: Ronald J Cockburn, 90 Ledi Drive, Bearsden. G461 4JW.
Journal: The True Line, usually published quarterly.
Web site: **www.crassoc.org.uk**

Glasgow & South Western Railway Association
Chairman: Ian Middleditch, Secretary: Andrew Munro
Membership: Graham Robinson, 4, Clochoderick Avenue, Kilbarchan, Refrewshire, Scotland PA10 2AY.
Journal: Sou' West Journal, usually published quarterly.
Web site: **www.gswra.org.uk**

North British Railway Study Group
Chairman: Jeff Hurst, Secretary: Mike Smith.
Membership: Mr. R. W. Lynn, 2 Brecken Court, Saltwell Road South, Low Fell, Gateshead, Tyne & Wear. NE9 6EY.
Journal: North British Railway Study Group, usually published quarterly.
Web site: **www.nbrstudygroup.co.uk**

Highland Railway Society
Chairman: Simon de Souza, Secretary: Ray Nolton.
Membership: John Fairlie, Winter Field, Terrys Lane, Cookham, Berkshire. SL6 9TJ.
Journal: Highland Railway Journal, usually published quarterly.
Web site: **www.hrsoc.org.uk**

Great North of Scotland Railway Association
Chairman: Keith G. Jones, Secretary: George Boardman.
Membership: R. P. Jackson, Craighall Cottage, Guildtown, Perth. PH2 6DF.
Journal: Great North Review, usually published quarterly.
Web site: **www.gnsra.org.uk**

Useful Web Sites.

This rapid growth area in recent years provides lots of on-line resources for Scottish Railway modellers. This list is not exhaustive as the Internet is very dynamic, new sites are being added daily. The inverse is also true, many sites, especially private ones, can quickly become defunct. However here is a selection to start with.

Scottish Model Railway Societies: many Scottish club site links can be found here - **www.modelrail-scotland.co.uk**
Infrastructure History: opening and closure dates and developments, plus latest news - **www.railscot.co.uk**
Preservation: happily there are many railway preservation societies in Scotland, a good starting point is the Scottish Railway Preservation Society, Bo'ness Station, Union Street, Bo'ness, West Lothian EH51 9AQ - **www.srps.org.uk**
The Borders: The Waverley Route Heritage Association, features some archive photographs - **www.wrha.org.uk**
Photos by Ernie Black: mainly the 1980s, but includes rare infrastructure shots - **www.rniescottishrailwayrchive.fotopic.net**
John Robin's Railway Photos: general views, many from 1960s - **www.john5798.fotopic.net**
Scottish Railway Photos: several private collections, mainly contemporary, can be accessed via - **srp.community.fotopic.net**

Stenlake Publishing. This company based in South West Scotland publish a huge range of historical photo albums. They include many which feature archive Scottish railway scenes, from early times up to the 1960s. Very informative and useful, their books are available direct by mail order via their website: **www.stenlake.co.uk** They also welcome visitors and customers to their office and retail premises at; Stenlake Publishing, 54-58 Mill Square, Catrine, Ayrshire, KA5 6RD. Scotland.

(ii) Locomotive Chronicle

One of the key questions modellers face in the quest for authenticity concerns locomotives: "which locos do I need for my chosen period?"

Scottish railways were little different from those in the rest of the UK. Locomotive development followed fairly similar patterns with, in the early days from the 1850s onwards, 2-4-0 types gradually giving way to 4-4-0 passenger types and 0-6-0 goods types, with 0-4-4T and 0-6-2T types for branch or suburban work. Although a generalisation, it rang true for the Scottish companies, such that by the dawn of the 20th Century, they were all using essentially these types, each to their own 'house design style', but with the engineers of the day keeping their eyes on what was going on over the fence. Each company had their own unique problems due to traffic patterns, or terrain, etc., and some notable unique designs emerged, such as the HR 'Skye Bogies' or the G&SWR 'Baltic' 4-6-4 tanks, but overall, the traction technology of the day was standard across the board.

An interesting observation is that the Drummond style of locomotive design permeated through many of the Scottish companies, such that by the latter part of the 19th Century, locomotives were emerging with distinctive 'Scottish' characteristics. A subjective notion of course, but there does seem to be a generic Scottish appearance amongst many of the pre-grouping designs. Many of them were very successful and survived through to the 1950s, with a few even beyond, and many of them appeared in British Railways liveries.

As a yard-stick for modelling purposes it would be reasonable to assume that pre-Second World War, many services were still in the hands of the pre-grouping designs. However, designs of English origin did appear after the 1923 grouping, although without great technological advance, examples of this were ex-Midland 2Ps (see page 47) and 'Compound' 4-4-0s, and a few 4Fs, mainly in ex-G&SWR and CR territory. Another phenomenon was the spread of certain pre-group designs, such as Caledonian 'Jumbo' 0-6-0 goods engines and 0-4-4 passenger tanks, well beyond their own 'patch' (see page 70).

The LNER adapted the GCR 'Director' class for service in Scotland and also transferred some ex-GER B12 4-6-0s to the GNoS section. Crabs began to be used initially on the ex-HR from around 1930 onwards, then after the Black 5s arrived there, circa 1934/5, they began their 32 year association with the ex-G&SWR. Royal Scot and Jubilee 4-6-0s too arrived from the 1920s on lines from Glasgow to the south, and Stanier's Princess and Duchess Pacifics on the West Coast Main Line. Likewise, the later designs of the LNER, such as the D49, K1, K3 and B1, filtered through as the years passed by, and the Gresley, Thompson and Peppercorn progression of Pacific designs appeared on the East Coast Anglo-Scottish route.

By the late 1950s the BR standard designs, tender and tank types, could be seen in areas where the pre-grouping designs had been withdrawn, though they did not become too widespread before diesels arrived. Nor did diesels appear overnight: they were phased in gradually from the late 1950s. In certain areas the transition did occur reasonably quickly: the West Highland and ex-Highland routes, for example, changed over promptly in 1962, such that steam and diesel traction were only occasionally seen together. The last steam in Scotland was in the Fife coalfield, and notably involved pre-grouping NBR 0-6-0s.

The Sulzer-engined Type 2 varieties are the most recognised for their Scottish Region internal duties and were highly successful in that role, in particular, the Class 26s and 27s on their respective patches are usually seen as 'archetypal', but the Class 24s and 25s were almost as widespread. A lesser success, spending almost their whole lives on Scottish metals, were the North British Locomotive Co. (NBL) Type 2s (see panel opposite). Another less successful type that became associated with lowland Scotland was the distinctive centre-cab Clayton Class 17; the last of these, and the NBL Type 2s, were withdrawn at the end of 1971.

Thus, various Type 1 and Type 2 designs became synonymous with the general Scottish Region scene in the 1960s and 1970s. A handful of Scottish-allocated Type 4s worked the internal Inter-City routes, but many others, together with the legendary Deltics, appeared on the Anglo-Scottish main line routes. Starting around 1975, the Type 2 classes were gradually withdrawn and by the mid 1980s, the few that were left were largely on departmental duties. The class 40s had gone by this time too, but cascading, due mainly to the introduction of new traction like HSTs and class 56s, had released more of the 1960s-built Class 37s and 47s from the English Regions. These reigned in Scotland for only a few short years on passenger duties, however: the arrival of the Classes 156 and 158 Sprinters, at the end of the 1980s, confined them principally to non-passenger work.

Today, most of the 37s and 47s have gone as well. In less than a century, the once enormous variety of locomotive types in Scotland has been whittled down to mainly two; 66s and 67s. A few BR designed 25kV locomotives still appear over electrified routes and the 1970s built HSTs can still be seen on Aberdeen and Inverness Anglo-Scottish services. Virtually all Scottish internal passenger services are now operated by the various second generation multiple unit types.

This is just a brief synopsis of Scottish locomotive history for use as a general guideline. Those wishing to be wholly accurate in their choice of period and stock will be able to undertake their own in-depth research in more specific publications.

The NBL Type 2s were introduced in 1959 and had a short and chequered career as mixed traffic locomotives. Later classified as Class 21, their problems were such that twenty were modified and re-engined, being re-classified as Class 29. Hornby's one-time model of the type is a bit of a hybrid, combining features of both the original class 21, and the rebuilds of class 29, but with a little work it can be turned into either. This typically thorough rework by Peter Johnson retains the headcode panel (as fitted to rebuilt locos), but has undergone other modifications to the side grilles and roof. An original loco would require a 'retro-fitted' disc headcode arrangement.

(iii) Signalling

By the later pre-Grouping period, all Scottish companies except the Highland were using lattice posts, supplied by Stevens of Glasgow.

There were however subtle detail differences between companies in the design of parts such as arms, lamps and finials. These signals survived intact on many routes (often with upper quadrant arms fitted from the 1930s) until either closure under the Beeching plan, or modernisation with tubular posts or colour light systems.

The Highland Railway used McKenzie and Holland slotted wooden posts (see Ardbealach, page 75), most of which had been replaced by BR days by lattice (different to the Stevens design) or tubular posts. HR ground signals were the standard McKenzie and Holland rotating type, with other companies all using the Stevens drop-flap design - again with slight detail differences between them. Replacement by LMS or LNER discs began in the late 1930s.

As always, research your chosen prototype and period for the signal styles and whether lower or upper quadrant arms were in use at the time. Model Signal Engineering offers a wide selection of parts for modelling Scottish signals, including complete kits in 4mm and 7mm scales for the upper quadrant versions of the CR, NB and G&SWR lattice post signals. For further details contact: MSE, PO Box 70, Barton upon Humber, DN18 5XY, **www.modelsignals.com**

(iv) Modelling Products and Suppliers

Modellers of the grouping, British Railways or post steam periods are well served for locomotive and stock models from the big manufacturers, especially in 4mm scale. The sourcing of models of pre-grouping prototypes is altogether different as reliance on kits is necessary. A few kit manufacturers that offer a retail service are listed below. There are also a few part-time manufacturers who produce kit parts, etched coach sides, etc., on a private arrangement basis by 'word of mouth'. Details of them can often be obtained through modelling groups and the Scottish Line Societies.

Falcon Brassworks, Llety Derwen, Llechryd, West Wales, SA43 2NL. Tel: 01239 682249. A good selection of HR locomotive kits, plus some CR and NBR types in 4mm, **www.ukmodelshops.co.uk/catalogues/falcon**
Mercian Models, 1A Market Way, Hagley, West Midlands, DY9 9LT. Tel: 01562 884800. A small selection of CR and G&SWR kits, mainly 4mm, but some availability in 7mm, **www.modelrailways.tv**
DJH Model Loco, Project House, Consett Business Park, Villa Real, Consett, Co. Durham, DH8 6B. Tel: 01207 500050. A good selection of HR, CR and NBR (1) locomotive kits in 4mm. Some kits offered built as R-T-R, **www.djhengineering.co.uk**
Caley Coaches, Jim Smellie, 15 Tay Crescent, Bishopbriggs, Glasgow, Scotland G64 1EU. A selection of 4mm Caledonian locomotive and stock kits, **www.caley.com**
Lochgorm Kits, 3 Broomhill Court, Keith, Banffshire, AB55 5EL Tel: 01542 886714. 4mm HR specialist, small selection of 4-4-0 locomotives, plus coach and wagon kits. Some 7mm parts, **www.lochgormkits.co.uk**
Connoisseur Models, 33 Grampian Road, Penfields, Stourbridge, DY8 4UE. A selection of 7mm kits of NBR prototypes including J83, J35, J36, J37, D32, C15, under the brand name **Claymore Kits.**
NB Models, 4 Earlston Way, Cramlington, Northumberland, NE23 3HP, A developing selection of NBR locomotive kits including C16, D29, D30, D34 in 7mm and N15 and J37 in 4mm, **www.nbmodels.com**
Shedmaster 0 Gauge Models, Gadebrook, 3 Green Lane, Hythe, Kent, CT21 4DY. Tel: 01303 269668. A few 7mm locomotive kits.
FourTrack Models, 22 Grange Road, Harrow, Middlesex, HA1 2PP. Tel: 020 8863 7338. Some 7mm items, **www.fourtrack.co.uk**
Scottish Scale Loco Works, individual hand-built locomotives in 0 Gauge and Gauge 1, **www.scottish-scale-loco-works.co.uk**

(v) Bibliography

There have been countless books published on Scottish Railways, covering the whole spectrum. Many are no longer in print but most public libraries can usually obtain copies to lend out. It is worth looking out at second-hand bookstalls for copies of such material too. An excellent starting point is the David and Charles long-established 'Regional History' series; Volume 6: the Lowlands and Borders, Volume 15: the North of Scotland.

The 'Forgotten Railways' series from the same publisher are also useful when researching the closed lines. Also the 'Trains Illustrated' range of locomotive profiles, have covered many of the Scottish railway company designs, and continue to do so with photographs showing a wealth of detail for modellers.

In this short bibliography I have included a selection of pictorial style books which are generally more suitable for layout building research, rather than pure historical reference works.

Steam in Scotland - 1: *W. J. V. Anderson and Derek Cross,* Ian Allan Ltd. 1968, ISBN 0 7110 0359 9.
Steam in Scotland - 2: *W. J. V. Anderson and Derek Cross,* Ian Allan Ltd. 1972, ISBN 0 7110 0386 6.
Scottish Steam: *W. J. V. Anderson, a tribute,* Ian Allan Ltd 2004, ISBN 0 7110 2992 X.
Scottish Steam in Colour: *Hugh Ballantyne,* Jane's Publishing Company 1987, ISBN 0 7106 0403 3.
Scottish Steam in Colour - 2: *Chris Gammell,* Ian Allan Ltd. 1993, ISBN 0 7110 2194 5.
The Heyday of the Scottish Diesels: *David Cross,* Ian Allan Ltd. 2002, ISBN 0 7110 2869 9.
Scottish Diesels, A Colour Portfolio: *David Cross,* Ian Allan Ltd. 2005, ISBN 0 7110 308 2 0
Scottish Urban and Rural Branch Lines: *Geo. C. O'Hara,* Eroxop Ltd. 1986, ISBN 0 9511417 0 8.
Scottish Region Colour Album No.1: *Geo. C. O'Hara,* Clyard Novella Ltd. 2003, ISBN 0 9530821 1 3.
Border Country Branch Line Album: *Neil Caplan,* Ian Allan Ltd. 1985, ISBN 0 7110 1086 2.
Highland Miscellany: *Peter Tatlow,* OPC 1985, ISBN 0 86093 309 1.
Highland Railway Album: *Anthony J Lambert,* Ian Allan Ltd. 1974, reprinted 1994, ISBN 1 85648 187 5.
North British Album: *A. A. Maclean,* Ian Allan 1976, ISBN 0 7110 0568 0.
Great North of Scotland Railway Album: *A. E. Glen, I. A. Glen and A. G. Dunbar,* Ian Allan Ltd., ISBN 1 85648 188 3.
Modelling the Great North of Scotland Railway: *Keith Fenwick,* GNSR Association, 1997, ISBN 902343 08.

Acknowledgments
The author and publisher would like to thank the following individuals and organisations for their help and assistance in the preparation of this book; R.W. Lynn, Allan Rodgers, W. A. C. Smith, George C. O'Hara, Roy M Crombie, Douglas Hume, Ian Middleditch, Stuart Rankin, Jeff Wetherell, Allan Goodwillie, Richard Heard, Andrew Hartshorne of Model Signal Engineering, Ian Fleming, Ken Gibbons, Neil A. Ripley, Graeme Elgar, Peter Johnson, Dave Skipsey, Mike Turner, Peter Goss.

Photographs appear; courtesy of Peco Publications and Railway Modeller (pgs; 1, 2, 74u, 75, 78u, 79, 87l), courtesy of the Great North of Scotland Railway Association (pgs; 25, 72), courtesy Wirral Finescale Railway Modellers (pgs; 37u, 69l), courtesy Geo. C. O'Hara and Clyard Novella Ltd. (pgs; 42c, 43, 51l, 52, 61c, 65l, 66c, 80u, 82, 98u, 98c). The scale drawing on page 71 appears by kind permission of the North British Railway Study Group.

Models and layouts featured, other than those of the author, appear courtesy of Adrian Walby (p.78), Dave Walker (p.79), Steve Flint (p.78), Bob and Gareth Rowlands (pgs; 50, 102), Nigel Bowyer (p.58), Peter Fletcher (pgs; 23, 75), Eddie Ford (p.29), Ian and Kenneth Middleditch (pgs; 23, 40 - 47), Trevor Hale and Tim Easter (p.58), Keith Fairweather (p.90), Allan Goodwillie, Rodger Pedrick and the East of Scotland 4mm group (pgs; 58, 60, 61), Jeff Taylor (p.66), Peter Johnson (pgs; 66, 73, 111), Paul Timperley (pgs; 2, 80).

Last words, field trips and library visits.

I remember when I commenced research into matters North British, there was very little available at the time, and a number of anomalies were created because certain details were not cross-checked or verified. In direct contrast, the amount of information that is available nowadays is quite astonishing: it simply takes a little bit of effort to find out about the issues that particularly interest you.

You can certainly gather historical evidence through books or photographs, but to explore the area you would like to model is, I firmly believe, the best way forward. Whilst not everyone is in a position to readily make site visits, such trips are invariably vital, and provide a means of absorbing the unique essence and atmosphere of a particular location. And this is still true even if the railway line or station has closed. Indeed, even if the route has long since gone, with little or no sign of earthworks or structures: just being there, and especially in Scotland, can be enough to allow you to 'catch' the very soul of the place. With the technology we have nowadays, photographs in particular are easy and cheap to produce and the Internet is readily available. If you are not connected to the Internet at home, a trip to most libraries will find plenty of computer terminals to work at.

Research is extremely rewarding and there are many people who will gladly assist you on your way. Many questions can be answered through books already published and unless you are interested in a small, remote railway company, which only ran for a short period, it is usually possible to find what you are looking for. Research does take time, but it is rewarding to unearth information or speak to others equally interested in your project. Good quality research should help us all to produce more accurate, and thus more distinctive model railways, even if at the end of the day, we do opt to include a little *modeller's licence* here and there. Here's to Scotland's Railways!
Ian Futers,
31st March 2006.